EDUCATOR'S GUIDE TO
Service Learning

SERVICE LEARNING, EXPERIENTIAL LEARNING, AND WHOLE-SCHOOL TRANSFORMATION

Br Damien Price

VAUGHAN PUBLISHING

The *Educator's Guides*

The Mission and Education Project of BBI-TAITE (The Australian Institute of Theological Education) includes a series of Guides designed to serve the educational mission of Catholic schools in Australia and beyond. The Guides introduce educators to ways in which mission and education may be integrated in the life and work of Catholic educators and students.

The mandate given to the expert writers who create these Guides is to tap into the best available treatments of mission, particularly as readily accessible from major Church documents, and also to ground their work in quality practice.

'Mission' in post-Vatican II Catholicism is a very rich concept. As baptised Christians we commit ourselves, individually and in community, to carry out the mission of Jesus in the world. This missional mandate takes us into some very demanding areas, calling for faith, expertise, prayer, and the support of our fellow Christians, as well as that of other partners beyond our communities.

We at BBI-TAITE are privileged to be at the service of the Church and offer these Guides as an element of that educational service.

Therese D'Orsa
Professor Mission and Culture
BBI-TAITE

Published in Australia by Vaughan Publishing
32 Glenvale Crescent, Mulgrave VIC 3170
A joint imprint of Garratt Publishing and BBI – The Australian Institute of Theological Education.

Copyright © 2021 Br Damien Price

All rights reserved. Except as provided by Australian copyright law, no part of this publication may be reproduced in any manner without prior permission in writing from the publisher.

Cover design and typesetting by Guy Holt
Images supplied by author: pp i, 5, 6, 8, 9, 10, 12, 14, 15, 16, 20, 21, 22, 23, 24, 25, 27, 28, 29, 31, 32, 33, 48 & cover
All other images supplied by iStock

The author and publisher gratefully acknowledge the permission granted to reproduce the copyright material in this book. Every effort has been made to trace copyright holders and to obtain their permission for the use of copyright material.

The publisher apologises for any errors or omissions in the above list and would be grateful if notified of any corrections that should be incorporated in future reprints or editions of this book.

ISBN 9780648524649

 A catalogue record for this book is available from the National Library of Australia

Nihil Obstat: Reverend Monsignor Peter J Kenny STD
Diocesan Censor
Archdiocese of Melbourne
Imprimatur: Very Reverend Joseph Caddy AM Lic.Soc.Sci VG
Vicar General
Archdiocese of Melbourne
Date: 28 July 2021

The *Nihil Obstat* and *Imprimatur* are official declarations that a book or pamphlet is free of doctrinal or moral error. No implication is contained therein that those who have granted the *Nihil Obstat* and *Imprimatur* agree with the contents, opinions or statements expressed. They do not necessarily signify that the work is approved as a basic text for catechetical instruction.

Br Damien Price provides a prophetic yet practical guide to service learning and experiential education. His wisdom distils over forty years of experience and innovation that is both compelling and inspiring for the staff, students and communities it seeks to challenge. Br Damien Price has produced an extraordinary resource that reveals the insights behind his proven track record to deliver individual and community transformation. Indeed, this guide is a 'must have' for educators from any context who wish to have a positive impact on students' academic outcomes, personal efficacy, spiritual growth and moral development.

Dr Conor Finn
Dean of Formation
Ambrose Treacy College

Br Dr Damien Price has made a significant, groundbreaking contribution to Service-Learning in the K – 12 Sector in Australia. His theological insights and wisdom challenges all to explore Service-Learning's significance and purpose in a variety of contexts. His doctoral research sheds light upon the psychological aspects of a conceptual approach to Service-Learning. His narratives-of-practice demonstrate the power of experiential learning. Br Damien has worked for a number of years supporting Service Learning Champions in differing school sectors. Amongst educators in Lutheran Schools he is an engaging and popular key-note speaker and workshop leader at whole-of-staff retreats, network meetings, post-graduate short-courses and at state-wide conferences. Br Damien's work is highly valued and has been a transformative influence for many.

Dr Meg Noack,
EdD, MEd, GradDipArts (Children's Lit), GradDipRE
Australian Lutheran College Sessional Lecturer/
University of Divinity

Br Damien Price's life has been dedicated to building global communities that allow people to live with dignity and choice. A key component of his work has been focused upon creating opportunities for people to immerse, listen and collaborate so that true community can be established. This lifelong passion has culminated in the formation of this book and challenges each of us to 'take off our blinkers' and to live with more presence and compassion.

Anthony Ryan
Chief Executive Officer Youngcare
Founder of Eddie's Van

Br Damien's work in the area of Service Learning gives heart to school culture and learning. His balance of research and practical application allows for a richness of engagement by both staff and students. Damien's capacity to engage the head, heart and hand and to inspire young people to serve community beyond the school gates is what education should be about.

Jodie Hoff, Principal LORDS
(Lutheran Ormeau Rivers District School)

It has been my privilege to know both the heart of the person, Damien, and the heart of the work he has been doing over many, many years. Br Damien Price cfc PhD is a rare teacher, an everyday prophet and a steadfast advocate for the many young men he has helped to grow into their own sense of being in the world. He has been at the leading edge of the work in Service Learning and Student Formation in Australia and it is wonderful to see this book bring to life his research, experience, passion and wisdom. This Guide is essential reading for all those educators involved in the structuring of service learning programs for students that are effective and sustainable with impact far beyond the school years.

Dr Jill Gowdie PhD GAICD
Founder and Director of Wisdom Works International

Census data indicate that Catholicism is in decline and 30% of Australians identify themselves as having no religion. Br Damien's book acknowledges this reality and offers reflective and pragmatic responses to assist students to serve those who hurt and who are ignored. Society's nobodies become somebodies to students, who commit themselves to service learning. The framework is a catalyst for the young to grow as caring humans, who want to make a difference to their slice of the world. If you can't recognise Jesus in the streets from Monday to Saturday, you sure won't on Sunday.

Assoc Professor Denis McLaughlin,
Australian Catholic University

Damien is a true champion in the field of Service Learning. I make this endorsement from both the perspective of adolescent student participant and adult learner, teacher, leader and facilitator in and of Service Learning. Whilst well intentioned efforts are often made in schools, striking the balance of mutual benefit, authentic participation, and embedded practice is not easy. Damien believes in the power of encounter through experience and deep and genuine connection with another. It is with his holistic approach that we move beyond simply participating, to having minds and hearts transformed – and for me it is in these moments that we experience 'fullness of life' (John 10:10).

Joshua O'Keeffe
Assistant Principal Religious Education
St Mary of the Cross, Windsor

Contents

Introduction	Service and the Gospel	1
Chapter 1	What is Service Learning?	4
Chapter 2	Psychological Processes within the Service Learning Experience	19
Chapter 3	The Power of Reflection	30
Chapter 4	Living into a Culture of Encounter	36
Chapter 5	Reflection and Engagement Techniques for the Practitioner	41
Conclusion	The Power and Possibility of Service Learning	47
Appendix	Service Learning Critical Questions	50
	Further Reading	54
	Helpful Terms	55
	About the Author	58

INTRODUCTION

Service and the Gospel

Modern humanity listens more willingly to witnesses than to teachers, and if they do listen to teachers, it is because they are witnesses.

Saint Pope Paul VI, *Evangelii Nuntiandi*, 1975

This Guide begins by asking, "What is Service Learning?" Sadly, Service Learning is one of the most misunderstood academic and professional pursuits within schools. Too many label one-off, isolated community support experiences as Service Learning. While there may be some element of service in these experiences, the true and potentially transforming power of Service Learning occurs when that experience is intimately linked to the culture and curriculum of the school community. Such a community becomes the 'cloud of witnesses' that Paul VI refers to in *Evangelii Nuntiandi*.

I would like to believe that it was no accident that on 14 October, 2018 Pope Francis canonised Pope Paul VI alongside Archbishop Oscar Romero. Both men, believing passionately in a better world for all, and in the missionary call of the Church to be an instrument for enabling this better world, were witnesses to the power of the Gospel. It was Paul VI who oversaw much of the Second Vatican Council after John XXIII had invited the Church to open wide its windows and engage with the people of God in the "joys and hopes, the griefs and the anxieties of the men of this age" (*Gaudium et Spes*, Pastoral Constitution on the Church in the Modern World). Romero, responding to the needs of the people of God in El Salvador, spoke out against poverty, systemic violence and injustice, and invited the people of God to be instruments for this better world for all. Many would claim that the following homily written by Bishop Ken Untener of Saginaw, Michigan, captured the heart and the spirit of Romero. He wrote:

This is what we are about.
We plant the seeds that one day will grow.
We water seeds already planted, knowing that they hold future promise.

We lay foundations that will need further development. We provide yeast that produces effects far beyond our capabilities. We can't do everything – there is a sense of liberation in realising that. This enables us to do something, and to do it very well. It may be incomplete, but it's a beginning, a step along the way, an opportunity for the Lord's grace to enter and do the rest. We may never see the end results, but that's the difference between the master builder and the worker. We are workers, not master builders, ministers, not messiahs. We are prophets of a future not our own.

Much of what inspired Paul VI and Romero also led Pope Francis to gift the Church and the world with his 2013 Apostolic Exhortation, *The Joy of the Gospel, Evangelii Gaudium*. In this Apostolic Exhortation Pope Francis says,

I prefer a Church which is bruised, hurting and dirty because it has been out on the streets, rather than a Church which is unhealthy from being confined and from clinging to its own security. I do not want a Church concerned with being at the centre and then ends by being caught up in a web of obsession and procedures.

(Pope Francis, *The Joy of the Gospel, Evangelii Gaudium*, p. 49.)

We live at a critical time in the history of the Church. In so many ways institutions, among them the Church, have lost so much credibility, especially in the eyes of the young. Young people are longing for meaning, for purpose, and to claim their agency as citizens for a new world (their civic identity) and their birthright by baptism as children of a loving God.

In this critical time the Catholic School stands out as a possible beacon in the darkness. While churches are emptying and ageing, and materialism and consumerism appear to be all pervasive, Catholic Schools are attracting an increasing number of families. These families are seeking an educational partnership that will not only skill their children for the life of commerce, but engage them in developing a worldview that will give their lives meaning.

It is in this context that Service Learning has so much to contribute.

After asking, "What is Service Learning?" Chapter 1 paints the background of Service Learning in the professional field of experiential education. Inspired by the work of Paulo Freire and John Dewey, Service Learning practitioners have continually refined the rich interplay between experience, reflection and learning. The latter sections of Chapter 1 introduce the reader to a model of Service Learning and invite them to reflect on how we learn, and especially the role that both Semantic and Episodic Memories play in this process. Semantic memory holds the internal 'map' we have developed over time by which we negotiate our everyday experiences. Episodic Memory is the immediate storage and sorting house that holds a particular experience. It is in the interplay between these two where new meaning-making happens and values and attitudes can change.

In Chapter 2 the psychological processes at play in quality Service Learning are unpacked, as it is an understanding of these processes that will enable the creation of program guides to lead participants to a more transformative level of experience within service. For Service Learning to be truly effective not only must it reflect the core values of the community, and be intimately linked to the curriculum and culture of the community, but it must also engage continuous reflection upon experience. Chapter 3 invites readers to engage with this reflection upon experience, as the personal worldview of participants will be engaged, challenged, and perhaps modified and transformed. It is in these processes that the hopes and dreams expressed by Paul VI, Romero and Pope Francis, come to life.

Chapter 4 provides a way to ensure deeper meaning-making linked to the experience students are having. It is through direct relationship with those we serve, time in service, the active engagement of program mentors, critical analysis, reflection upon experience and wrapping the whole dynamic in a credible theology and spirituality, that participant's worldview is hopefully expanded and transformed, and students learn to live into a 'culture of encounter'.

Chapter 5 offers a range of best practice techniques for student reflection and engagement. These are invaluable for the service learning practitioner. (Appendix A places before us a series of critical analysis questions that will assist in unpacking understanding linked to experience.)

The guide concludes by affirming the power and possibility of Service Learning in assisting educational practitioners bring about the reign of God within our world.

Our goal in every Catholic School ought to be to graduate students with the core values and associated concepts of that school deeply understood and owned. When experiences of a core value are woven through the culture, curriculum and Service Learning program of a school, and these experiences are reflected upon, then that value will be deeply internalised.

This dynamic applies especially to the learnings of our heart – our values and beliefs. This dynamic is at the very heart of what we are doing in Service Learning. When we experience and reflect upon our experience through the lens of our values and beliefs, we learn and grow.

It will be this kind of internalising and ownership of core values that will mission the student forth, not only deeply aware of their baptismal call to make a difference but also aware of their personal agency to do so.

As we begin the journey of engagement in an authentic process for Service Learning, the diagram following provides a map of the student journey. Use this map as you reflect on your own school or college community's capacity to enrich your student's world view in the transformational work of Service Learning.

Note: During this guide many direct quotations are used from students reflecting on their experiences of working with and building relationships with the homeless. These quotations are linked to Eddie's Van, a ministry of St Joseph's College, Gregory Terrace in Brisbane. **The coloured photos used in this guide are used with permission from St Joseph's College, Gregory Terrace. The black and white photos are used with permission of the photographer, Mr Chris Rix.**

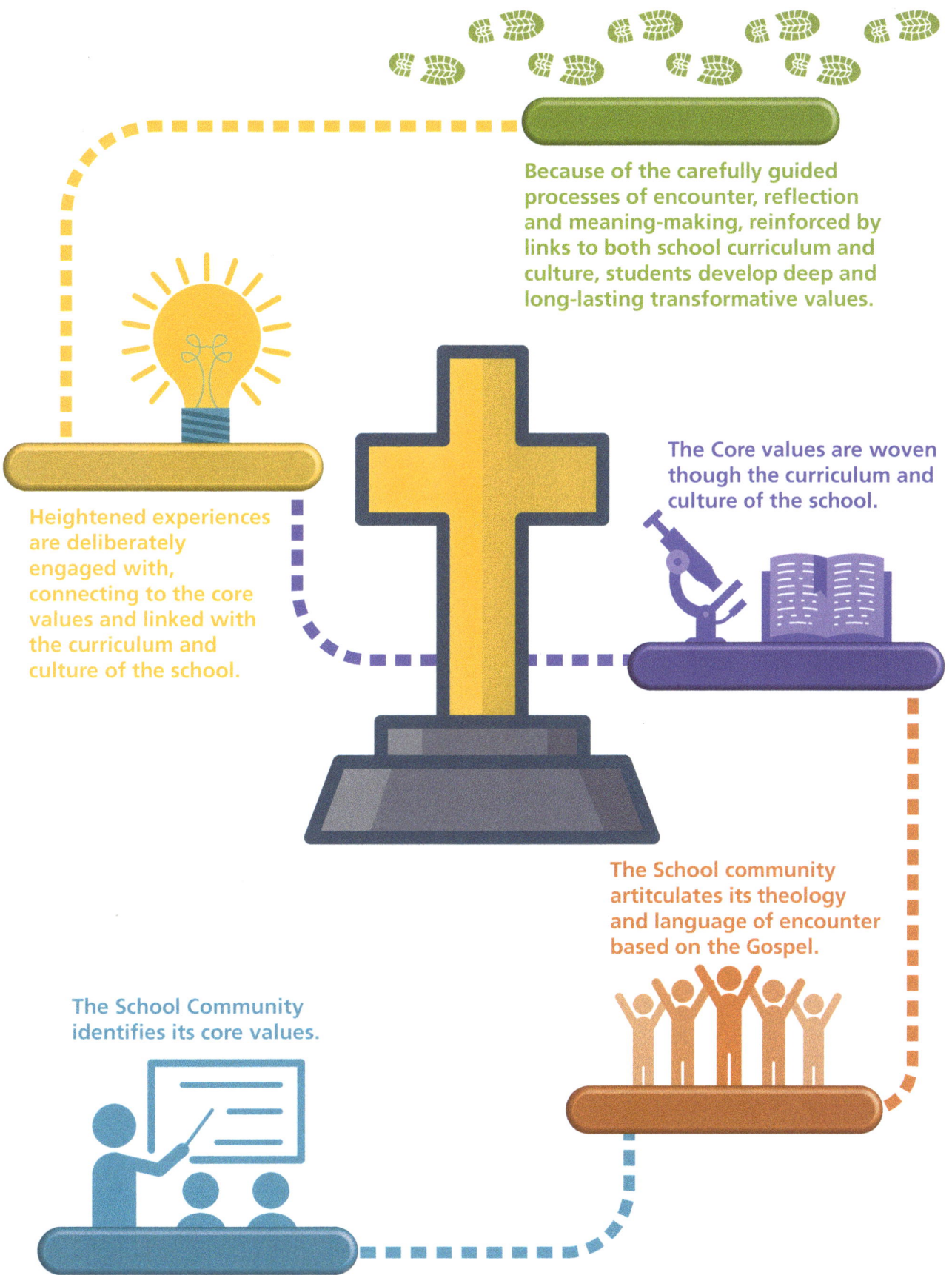

CHAPTER 1
What is Service Learning?

I was chatting to Len, a homeless guy that I knew well. He came over to me quite disturbed. He told me to be careful as "they were watching us, they have cameras everywhere!" "Who are watching us Len?" "They are, the Government, the City council, the army, they are everywhere, they are on the top of every building and they have cameras watching our every move!" For the rest of that time Len was sharing with me his fears and the fears we should all have as our every move was watched. At one point, a small voice in my head clicked in, "Len is crazy, he has lost the plot!" Then almost as quickly another voice in my head came into play, "No this is just Len's mental illness, it is part of his paranoia, part of his story of abuse and substance abuse and resultant mental illness. I will just be present to Len, to his story, to him beyond the presenting mental illness!

Journal reflection from James on Eddie's Van

The journal reflection above points to the value of Service Learning. In this instance, James has deeply encountered Len, one of the homeless men who lived in a park in inner city Brisbane. What had James learned? James' initial response that Len was crazy was very quickly reframed in the context of the core values of his Service Learning program and the content of the relevant curriculum. James has learned about mental illness and substance abuse through curriculum input. James then placed this curriculum framing into the context of the school's values, including the innate dignity of every person, their story and their presence, and our presence to the person as distinct from their presenting behaviour. Such learning is liberating and deeply influenced James' worldview.

While the reflection above is significant it also points to a major difficulty facing Service Learning – that is a tendency to equate Service Learning only with powerful encounters such as that which James experienced. This guide would suggest that James' was a heightened experience that was truly transformative but one that very few in a school community would have the opportunity to experience. For Service Learning to reach its fullest potential within an educational community it must consist of both heightened experience (deliberate and targeted experience associated with our core values) and normative experiences (experiences woven through the day-to-day fabric of the school community that reflect our core values).

> Service Learning is when, as part of its curriculum and culture, the members of a school community are invited to engage directly and indirectly in service experiences with the wider community. Through reflection upon their experience associated with the core values of the community, participants are challenged to evaluate or modify their worldview.

This guide deliberately takes a holistic view of Service Learning. This first chapter of our study guide helps the reader to be clear as to what Service Learning is, and its worth and place in educational theory.

For an activity to be Service Learning it must be both 'service' and 'learning'. Many communities show this by expressing the term using a hyphen; Service-Learning.

Experiential Learning

The theoretical home for the approaches undertaken in this guide can be found in the work of Paulo Freire and John Dewey. Freire's work challenged a 'jug-mug' approach to education with his emphasis on a dialogical approach to the learning dynamic.

Paulo Freire

For Freire, dialogue in the learning dynamic had to be based upon respect, not "one person acting on another, but rather people working with each other". In *Pedagogy of the Oppressed* Freire is critical of a 'banking' approach to learning where the educator makes deposits in the one being 'educated'.

Of particular importance for our work here, Freire was deeply concerned with praxis – where action is informed and linked to certain values. Freire's approach to learning not only sought to deepen understanding within the student but to lead them to be part of making a difference in the world through dialogue and cooperative activity that involves respect. This awareness of one's ability and call to make a difference in our world we will refer to as agency.

John Dewey

The American educationalist and philosopher John Dewey, writing in the 1930's, was passionate about reflected upon experience as being a prime facet of true learning. Dewey experimented with the links between experience, inquiry and reflection. But this experimentation always took place in the context of society, and the civic identify of youth taking their place in society with a sense of their own agency. So, while Dewey was concerned with how learning took place and what the learning actually was, he was focused on asking how that learning led to action within society.

Dewey's great contribution that has significantly influenced Service Learning is insight into the power and importance of reflection on experience.[1]

The Power and Potential of Service Learning

The power and potential of Service Learning is reflected in James' journal entry that began this chapter. James came to insights about mental illness and about the power of presence to a depth that he may never have reached through simply listening to a guest speaker or reading about homelessness in a book. Furthermore, James' insights about mental illness and presence will hopefully remain with him on his life's journey.

Service

Service Learning first requires that the action be one of service. This service brings about the reign of God, a more just and whole experience of life to the full for all.

---

1 Giles & Eyler, 1994.

In Service Learning in schools, the school community will break open the concept of service and ensure that the student does not see it as charity or giving.

Other-centred encounter

Service is intimately linked to the culture of encounter that Pope Francis frequently refers to. The service encounter is a reciprocated encounter in which one both gives and receives. And it is respectful in that it focuses on the innate dignity of the one encountered and liberating in that it in some way frees both parties to the encounter.

Service is other-centred and in the paradox of the Gospel it gifts the one who serves. Service will enhance the quality of life of all involved in the encounter. However, service is not necessarily about fixing or even helping. Certainly in the other-centred encounter the one who serves may also assist the other. But ultimately in the service encounter you come as a guest to the sacred space and story of the other, you choose to be deeply present, and you allow your heart to open in compassion.[2]

Service needs to be engaged within a broad understanding. Too many images of Jesus washing the feet of his disciples come to mind, and while that image from the Gospel of John is a great compass point for us, it is only one understanding of service. Perhaps it may be better to see service as an 'other centred' encounter whether the other be the earth itself, the elderly, the stranger, the differently abled, a minority group or even our peers.

Service does not stand alone

The Service we are speaking about reflects and links in to the culture, curriculum and core values of the community. Service does not stand alone nor is it a one-off 'feel good' experience. When a school community is engaging in an experience of service that is in isolation from the curriculum and/or culture of the community it can do harm, ingrain stereotypes, enhance dualistic thinking and undermine the core values of the community.

The experience of service that the community deliberately and professionally engages with will be clearly linked to aspects of the curriculum and or culture of the school. A unit of work in Biology may result in the experience of regeneration of an area of bushland overtaken by weeds and introduced species. A unit of work in Language Arts focusing on biography and storytelling may find the class interviewing students from a refugee school and together engaging in a creative writing piece. A unit of work in Geography focusing on liveability may result in students building relationships with homeless people and growing in their appreciation of the concept of cause and effect.

2   Nouwen, 1975.

The Service Learning Space

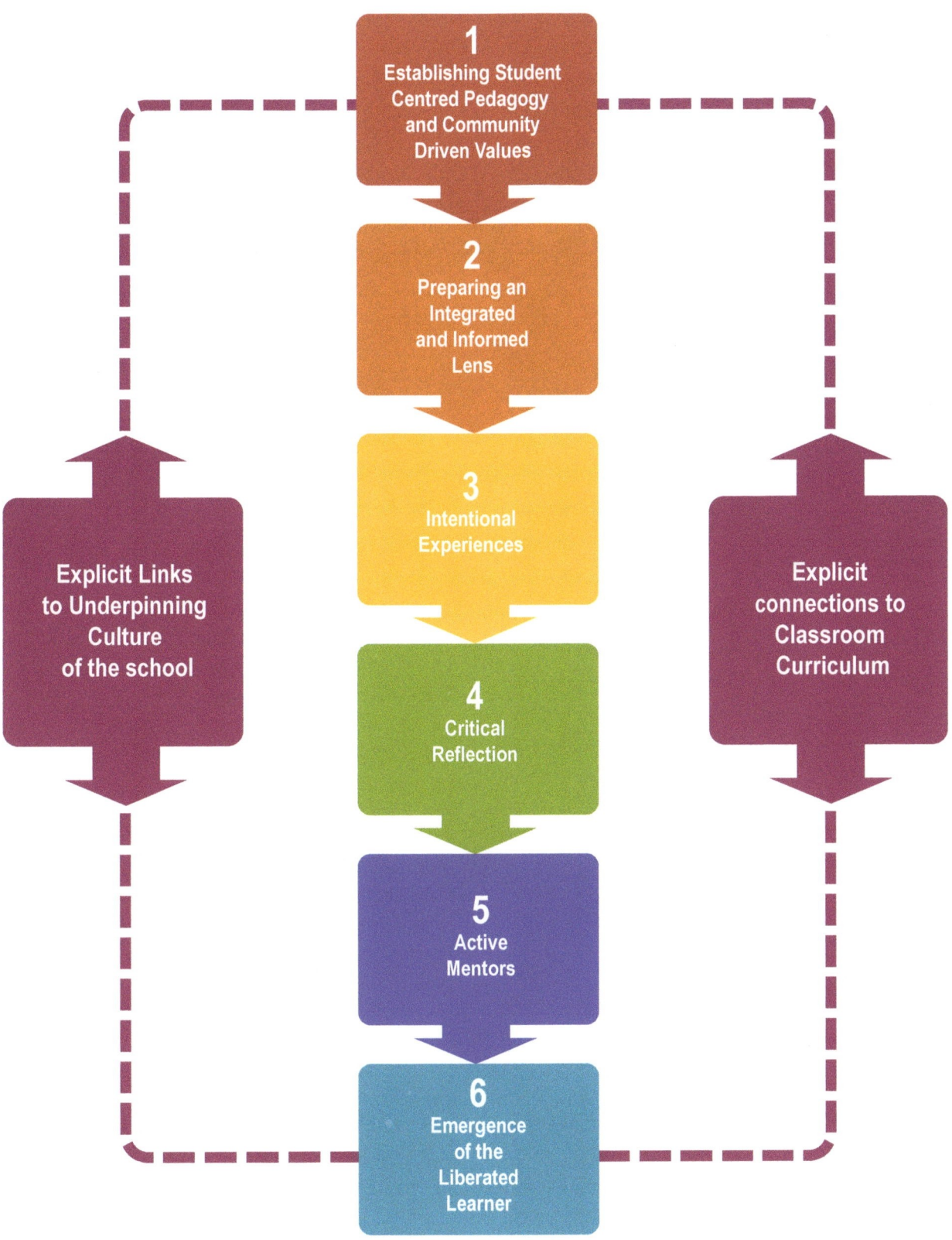

Learning

The distinguishing feature of Service Learning however lies in the learning aspect of these encounters. We desire for the encounter to be transformative, to challenge, modify and/or change our worldview. Learning occurs when a concept placed in Semantic Memory is experienced in Episodic Memory and that experience is then reflected upon.

The learning in Service Learning will be aligned to a deliberate engagement with particular curriculum content. Using the Biology example cited previously, a teacher may engage with students in a unit of work that breaks open the content around ecosystems, interdependence and interconnectedness. When this content is then taken to students to research what types of plants and shrubs should be purchased or grown to regenerate an area of land, and then the students are actually engaged in the planting and upkeep of these plants and shrubs, learning occurs at a deeper and more transformative level.

Of course, concepts such as interdependence and interconnectedness can be applied in many other areas of the curriculum, and would deeply link to an understanding of what Pope Francis was inviting us to through his encyclical *Laudato Si*. Service Learning invites a creative approach to both the school curriculum and culture. This approach asks for much lateral thinking, but gifts the learning process with great potential for transformation and worldview.

In many ways Service Learning, when allied with other aspects of experiential learning and when linked to ritual and symbol, forms community, and promotes acceptance and welcome. All this leads to a communal sense of mission which can be where the 'rubber hits the road' in Catholic schooling.

Service Learning is closely linked to our sense of mission. Service Learning equips students with a profound sense of their own agency (their ability to make a difference) and a sense of their civic identity: and associated with this a sense of being Church for our world.

Service Learning can contribute much to the Catholic Identity of the school. For youth in their adolescent years setting out on the adventure of developing a sense of their own identity, challenging boundaries and seeking meaning and purpose, Service Learning can be one of the primary contexts in which this adventure can unfold.

Service Learning that strengthens the Catholic Identity of schools has the following characteristics:

1. Service Learning is underpinned by the Gospel principles highlighted in the *Church's social justice documents*.

2. Service Learning must be experienced over an *extended period of time*. Having one-off experiences does not reflect best practice nor nurture deep and transformative learning.

3. Service Learning includes processes of *briefing and debriefing*, both of which are highly reflective.

4. Connecting Service Learning to *the broader Jesus story* transforms the experience from secularised goodwill to strengthening the Catholic identity of a school.

5. Service Learning is *connected explicitly to the curriculum and culture* within a Catholic school or College. Service Learning, along with retreats, immersions and outreach activities, forms part of an integrated student formation plan in every Catholic school (Brisbane Catholic Education guidelines).

The Mission of the Catholic school is beautifully reflected in Service Learning. When the faith community identifies its core values and these find expression in the culture, curriculum and Service Learning program of the school, we create a synchronicity across all aspects of school life that has integrity and speaks to the heart of what we are about.

When the values and concepts inherent in the Service Learning experience (reflecting the core values of the school) are broken open with students, experienced within the heightened experience and then reflected upon, deep learning occurs. When these processes occur regularly and become part of the culture of the school, Service Learning can contribute significantly to worldview change and personal transformation. Service Learning can truly be the Gospel in Action.

The Service Learning model shown above is linear and as such does not reflect accurately the spiral nature of service and particularly of learning linked to service. The model is based upon the Lens Model of Cone and Harris.[3]

The Service Learning Model

In this next section of the guide the stages of the model are broken open. Too many schools go straight to the 'Experiences' section of the model, thus tending to disconnect the experiences of students from the overall learning dynamic. However, fundamental to an authentic and effective Service Learning model is an engagement with each aspect of the model.

---

[3] Cone & Harris, 1996, p. 45.

Stage 1

Establishing Student Centred Pedagogy and Community Driven Values

The Service Learning program must be student centred. Each student comes to the Service Learning experience with their own personal history, value systems, perspectives, attitudes, expectations and cognitive abilities. The goal of Service Learning is to engage with the student's values and attitudes and walk with them through their engagement with experiences. This will hopefully lead to that same student graduating from/moving on from their experience with newly integrated values and concepts that will impact the way they see the world. The most effective Service Learning programs are where the community has clearly articulated its values and ensured these pervade the curriculum, culture and Service Learning program.

It is surprising how often Service Learning experiences are framed in isolation to the core values of a school.

Stage 2

Preparing an Integrated and Informed Lens

It is just as surprising how often each experience is framed without the deliberate framing of core values and concepts.

How do we learn from an experience?

It was Pope Paul VI who in 1975 voiced the truth that modern humanity listens more willingly to witnesses than to teachers, and if they do listen to teachers, it is because they are witnesses! The witness has experience! There is something powerful in the reflections of the Chinese Confucius devotee Xunzi when he said, "Not hearing is not as good as hearing, hearing is not as good as seeing, seeing is not as good as knowing, knowing is not as good as acting; true learning continues until it is put into action!"

Effective service learning develops and embeds new ways of seeing the world through specific and carefully structured experiences. Changing the way we think, or even simply growing out of our unconscious assumptions, requires a deliberate engagement with concepts linked to an experience and reflection upon that experience. Our memory is like a storehouse. Within it are the mind-maps that I've drawn from all my life experiences, the things I know that create paths to help me navigate the new things I encounter. The Memory Storehouse is the Semantic Memory. The Memory Moment focuses on the immediate experience and its associated feelings, connections and thoughts. The Memory Moment is the Episodic Memory. We learn when a concept or thought, challenge or data, is introduced to our Semantic Memory, experienced in Episodic Memory and then reflected upon.

If I am travelling to a new destination and am not sure of how to get there, I first get out a map or type it into a search engine or speak to someone who knows the way. I then experience the journey to that destination, noting the landmarks and internally noting the length of the journey, the time of day, the levels of traffic and more. All of these are experienced in my Episodic Memory which is in constant interplay with Semantic Memory. Once I have arrived at the destination and reflected on the journey,

I have now grown new awareness or knowledge in my Semantic Memory; but it is still not necessarily learned.

If I repeat that journey several times – retrieving from Semantic Memory, continuing to be assisted by maps and other aids and noting again and again landmarks and other data, and each time reflecting on the experience held in Episodic Memory – then that journey gradually becomes learned. The day comes when I have learnt how to get to that destination. It is now deeply part of my Semantic Memory.

Forming Semantic Memory

We prepare the Memory Storehouse (Semantic Memory) by populating it with a rich variety of concepts, reflection, analytical skills, relevant curriculum content, and experience of the culture of the community. In Service Learning, these factors reflect the core values of a community. All Service Learning theorists speak of the importance of this phase of the Service Learning framework or model.

Semantic Memory will be populated and prepared for the service experience by:

a. *remaining focussed on student needs*

b. *identifying the core values (and associated concepts) of the community*

c. *curriculum and cultural mapping of the identified core values and concepts and ensuring they frame all that the teaching community does*

d. *identifying normative experiences in the day-to-day curriculum and culture that engage with the core values and concepts*

e. *identifying heightened Service Learning experiences that will deliberately engage the core values and concepts*

f. *identifying and planning links between heightened experience and relevant curriculum content and culture.*

Briefing

Program mentors are used to spending time briefing the students for the experience itself. This briefing time is essential for psychological safety but also for effective learning. The goal of the brief is to awaken the conscious awareness of the students during their experience through the lens' of the core concepts and values. Two important aspects of this will be anticipatory and active cognition.

> Anticipatory cognition is where the language, concepts and approaches that are to frame an encounter focus the awareness energy just prior to the encounter. Active cognition occurs when those same elements are triggered in the encounter moment.

In the following instance James anticipates 'guest-ness' within an encounter and then activates and experiments with the concept in the midst of the service experience.

> *One morning on Eddie's Van I looked over and saw James sitting on the ground next to a homeless man who was on a bench. I observed this encounter weekly for three weeks and noticed that there was some conversation and James would occasionally get up and get the man a coffee or breakfast roll. The third time I observed the interaction I noticed James was sitting on the bench next to the man. I inquired of him, "What was going on?" James referenced our work in the classroom where we spoke about the importance of coming as 'guest' to an encounter. James shared with me, "The man was a bit of a loner. He was choosing to sit over to the edge of the space on his own. This was his turf, his space. I had to come as guest to him and build up trust slowly. That is why I chose to sit on the ground at first. After three weeks I introduced myself and he shared his name with me!"*
>
> Based on the journal reflection of James on Eddie's Van.

Program theology and spirituality

Essential to the formation of an informed lens, Semantic Memory and the briefing will involve the framing of the anticipated experience around the school's theology and spirituality.

For the school with a focus on the Gospel of Jesus, the theology and spirituality that underpins the Service Learning program will provide a ladder to a possible profound encounter with the 'mystery we call God!' One simple approach to such a theology would entail:

a. Coming to the encounter with the other as a **'guest'**. The guest comes slowly and respectfully with an open heart. As a 'guest' is HOW we come to the encounter.

b. In the encounter space we make a deliberate choice to be deeply **present**.

c. We are present to the **innate dignity** of the other. In Christian theology we refer to the other as the temple of God's Holy Spirit.

d. When we approach the encounter in this way our hearts will naturally open in empathy and **compassion**.

e. Both persons in the encounter (and the Earth itself) come away from that sacred space **liberated**.

Truly Service Learning reflects the often-quoted words of St Teresa of Avila, "Christ has no body now but yours!" What is outlined also reflects the dynamics present in the encounters that filled Jesus' days.

> *I tried to be present while the homeless people were talking. I tried to remember a conversation that will enable me to start/ continue the conversation on the next outing.*
>
> Journal reflection from Colin on Eddie's Van.

This approach will both be a ladder and a lens assisting students to go ever deeper into meaning-making through their reflections. The journal entries by Colin and Wade reflect their use of the spirituality of the program when encountering people living on the streets.

> *I tried to make their day. I tried to 'come as a guest' even more and forget about the little things that annoy me.*
>
> Journal reflection from Wade on Eddie's Van.

Compromise

Sadly, the preparation of Semantic Memory is the element of Service Learning that too many schools ignore. Too often the Service Learning program is a set of 'experiences' engaged in by students, sometimes only a select few, and separate to the curriculum and culture of the community. This approach removes much of the learning from Service Learning. Moreover, it compromises our goals of worldview change to ensure that the Christ-centred community is at the service of the reign of God within our world.

Stage 3
Intentional Experiences

Types of Experience

There are two basic types of experience linked to Service Learning within the curriculum and culture of a community: normative and heightened experiences. One of the dangers of Service Learning is that we pigeonhole it to be associated with a number of boutique experiences that only a small cohort of students will ever know. This approach to Service Learning often supports a dualistic belief that service is separate from day-to-day life and is for only a select few.

Normative Experiences

The great potential of Service Learning begins to be realised when it finds expression in a myriad of smaller experiences woven through the culture and the curriculum of the school, and is deliberately linked to the core values of the school. These smaller experiences are what we refer to as normative experiences. These normative experiences are essential for the success of a community in its endeavours to effectively transmit its deeply held values to the members of their community.

The diagram on this page shows the normative experience where the core values of the community is experienced in the day-to-day culture and curriculum of the school.

The normative experience takes the value or concept beyond the extraordinary and into the day-to-day. The normative experience may take the form of a simulation game, a guest speaker, a ritual at an assembly, a Skype interview with someone from a majority world country or in-depth analysis of data from a field trip.

Heightened Experiences

There is a great value in weaving through our curriculum and culture heightened experiences that deliberately and specifically address specific values and concepts. We use the term 'heightened experience' because within the experience the student's awareness levels are heightened to focus on particular stimuli, reflection activities are more specifically targeted, and the experience itself more focused and deliberate.

These heightened experiences allow us the time and the professional space to unpack a value or concept, focus it, depth it and reinforce what the student is already experiencing in the day-to-day life of the school. The heightened experiences that a community would engage with would be linked to:

- the core values of that community
- the needs of the curriculum
- the needs of the students and the skill set of the teachers.

Examples of a heightened experience may include:

a. immersion Experiences – locally and globally
b. special days such as a tree planting day
c. elements of school excursions
d. special community events such as a grandparents' day
e. special community rituals

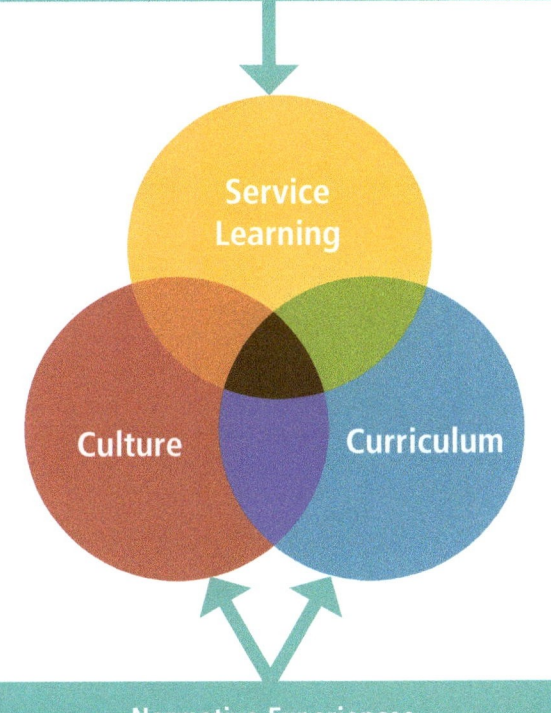

Normative and Heightened Experiences within the School Community

Heightened Experiences
Characterised by: strategic, heightened arousal; a focus on particular stimuli, and targeted experiences; all deliberate and specifically linked to core values.

Service Learning · Culture · Curriculum

Normative Experiences
Smaller, short term experiences in the day-to-day life of the community linked to core values.

f. retreats and reflections times

g. key networks and relationships, for example with a local pre-school or nursing home

h. service activities such as volunteering at a soup kitchen or homeless shelter, or working on a street van

i. holiday camps for children from marginal communities.

The Service Learning program will include a variety of experiences that hook the student's growing civic identity, their need for agency, and their psychological needs as they grow towards adulthood.

Stage 4

Critical Reflection

The quality of reflection on experience is key to the effectiveness of Service Learning. It is important that reflection is user friendly and nuanced both to reflect student need and the nature of the experience. Sadly, in the busyness of schools the reflective element of service is often overlooked or merely given lip service.

Episodic Memory

> Episodic Memory (or Memory Moment) is the immediate storage and sorting house that the actual service experience and the emotive reactions to that experience are stored in.

Because we have engaged Stage 2 well (the preparation of an integrated and informed Semantic Memory lens) the student now has all they need for effective learning and meaning-making.

During the Critical Reflection stage the student will be reflecting on practical aspects of the encounter, storing the immediate experience in their Episodic Memory, and also making meaning and analytic links with concepts and content in their Semantic Memory.

Reflection styles and activities will mirror the skill set of the professional mentor leading the experience. Ideally a wide variety of reflection techniques will be used to engage each student's style. These may include:

- responding to photo language
- journaling
- word association

---
4 Youniss & Yates, 1997, p. 33.

- development of cause-and-effect matrices from student reflections
- role play
- art

and much more. The key is to ensure that the reflection medium is attuned to the facets of the experience, reflects student needs, and engages the mentor's skill set. Approaches to reflection are broken open further in Chapter 5.

Social Analysis

Another aspect of reflection upon experience is Social Analysis. Social analysis skills need to be taught as part of the curriculum of the school. Social analysis hooks the natural emerging adulthood energy and the agency energy of youth. Our youth want to be part of a community that is making a difference in our world. They want to be 'makers of history'.[4] Some questions linked to social Analysis form Appendix A at the conclusion of this guide.

As part of their making sense of the causal factors linked to an experience program, mentors will continually remind students that they need to come as a guest to their analysis and questions, holding them lightly.

Program mentors will, as part of social analysis, invite students to become aware of:

Personal and Structural Attribution

> Personal Attribution is where the student assigns responsibility for the presenting circumstances to personal attributes such as laziness.

The following journal reflection from Rory is a personal attribution which provides program mentors with great material for deeper reflection upon experience.

What I still have trouble with understanding is why some of these people are on the street. The council has a myriad of programs available to help these people get off the streets into low-cost accommodation. So why are there still perfectly sane healthy people out on the street?

Journal Reflection from Rory on Eddie's Van

> Structural Attribution is where the student reframes responsibility for life circumstances to societal structures and community attitudes, or aspects of life's journey that the person had little or no control over. Structural Attribution will continually point to the complexity of causal issues linked to poverty in all its forms.

Below Ben and Malcolm engaged in Structural Attribution.

The guy I was talking to studied a lot in school and did well. He was a single child and his father died when he was 12 and his mother left after his dad had died. He was then confused and did not know what to do, so he ended up on the streets. As he was very dependent upon his parents, he had not developed any skills or [had] any support, he had no money at this stage.

Journal reflection from Ben on Eddie's Van.

I've only seen this guy once and he just [kept] talking about all the things that have happened to him on the street and I think he had a pretty bad gambling addiction and he was adopted as a child so he was not really settled in his home kind of thing. It was just a series of things that sort of led to where he was now. But as our teachers say, there is probably something there but I could not see it easily …

Journal reflection from Malcolm on Eddie's Van.

Stage 5

Active mentors

Program mentors must be actively involved in learning dynamics with students. This involvement will firstly be from a duty-of-care point of view but also with a focus on the 'learning' within the encounter. A quality Service Learning program will not tell students what they should think or believe, nor do the thinking for them, but program mentors are actively involved in the learning dynamic. Program mentors will:

- Be actively involved in duty of care elements of the program.

- Be conscious of trigger events that may occur for a student and engage in reflection around these events with those students.

- Sense the level of readiness participants have for varying levels of reflection on experience and respond to this.

- Ask the 'left-field' question.

- Introduce new stimuli to enhance a particular experience.

- Focus the attention of students onto particular facets of the experience.

- Continually monitor the level of reflection upon experience and ensure that normalisation is being challenged.

- Ensure that Semantic Memory is populated with real and relevant curriculum material, and the core concepts particular to that experience.

- Ensure that the elements of the experience encountered in their Episodic Memory will lead to and enhance the learning outcomes hoped for.

- Join with other members of the staff community to ensure effective mapping of the core values of the Service Learning program within the curriculum, and the culture of the community.

- Assist fellow educational professionals in making effective curriculum and cultural links to the Service Learning program.

Stage 6

Emergence of the Liberated Learner

No program mentor is Superman or Wonder Woman and no Service Learning program will win the Nobel Prize, but our energy for involvement is to be part of the journey to assist young adults claim their place in making it a better and more just world for all. This is the imperative of the Gospel. This is our mission.

Cone and Harris (1996) conclude their Lens Model for Service Learning with, "Learners with newly integrated concepts and modified world view." This is the goal of Service Learning. We seek to graduate learners from their journey within our community or from an individual experience (especially a heightened experience) with newly integrated concepts and some degree of worldview change. Our core values and associated concepts such as pilgrim, tourist, acceptance, guest, presence, dignity, power, home, story and more will have changed and deepened. The founder of my Religious Congregation, Blessed Edmund Rice, once said, "Have courage, the good news will grow up in the children's hearts later on!"[5] At times the sought-after integration and worldview change may not be immediately apparent; we need to trust the process and the web of caring, and trust the professional relationships that make up our community.

Worldview

Scott Seider's (2007) work specifically addressed the importance of a Service Learning program engaging with students' worldview modifications. Sometimes the Service Learning program will seek to replace a previous worldview and motivate students to claim their agency and call to 'make a difference'. On other occasions the Service Learning program will provide students with a long term means to be of service and this journey will, in turn, modify their worldview. There will be times when the experiences within a program focus the students' energy on particular aspects of society, and especially the structural injustice so often present within society. This will, in itself, provide a sharpened focus for students long after the initial experience has concluded.

Our young people are often idealistic. Many of them are ready to claim their agency within our world. The recent global climate strikes, the Me-Too movement and protests around Black Lives Matter all point to the energy and agency of youth. This energy is nothing new and every generation has witnessed young people raise their voices in their own way in protest against the injustices of their day. The role of the educational professional is not to be fearful of this adolescent energy but to work with it, enable it and channel it to a depth of reflection linked to our core values that will make a long-term difference.

A challenge for all our educational communities will be to bridge the school-post-school divide. Too often we inspire and invite our young people to make a difference within their world, and when they respond we do not have the vehicles to make a difference available for them. By developing the strong, values-based links described in this guide between curriculum, culture and Service Learning, we will create a tradition of service within our communities that will be all pervasive and give our communities great authenticity.

More importantly we will gift the students with skills and a worldview that they will take with them into the marketplace of life.

---

5   Normoyle, 1977, p. 500.

The Service Learning Phases

CHAPTER 2
Psychological Processes within the Service Learning Experience

I loved meeting Ram again and we just walked up to each other and greeted each other like old friends. Ram sleeps in the Botanical Gardens and I first met him on the 22nd of April. When I first met him he was very quiet, looking down at the ground asking, "What have you got?" And I was trying to get deeper asking have you seen this or that? This time he and I walked up to each other and greeted each other like old friends. I immediately sensed he had changed. He was looking at me eye to eye and speaking louder and more confidently. He and I talked about ANZAC day and other things. It was gratifying to see that I had become a friend to a man who needed friendship.

Journal reflection from Mark on Eddie's Van.

Identity Journey

If we are to provide best practice in Service Learning in the context of a transformative school community then we need to understand, from a psychological point of view, what is going on for the participant. For example, in Mark's reflection above he is engaging in the process of personalisation whereby Ram is now a person with a name, personality, story and all the hallmarks of a day-to-day relationship.

When we engage young people in experiences linked to the core values of our community we are:

- Engaging with them in the identity journey that all adolescents walk. In particular we are engaging with their civic identity.

- Aiming to enhance a person's personal sense of agency so that they believe "I can make a difference!"

- Aiming to grow a sense of mission so that part of a person's civic identity and their call from the Gospel is to be sent forth to make a difference in our world.

- Aware that each participant brings their unique personality, life story and worldview to the service space.

- Are aware that no two participants will have the identical 'experience' and hence meaning-making response linked to the heightened experience.

Phases within the heightened experience

Each heightened experience has varying phases that the participant will go through. Generally participants, especially if the experience is over several days (similar to an immersion) or regularly over several months (e.g., volunteering to visit a refugee school over the length of a term), will experience the following phases linked to their experience:

1. Expectations Phase
2. Exposure Phase
3. Reframing Phase
4. Disillusionment Phase
5. Awareness Phase
6. Agency Phase

1. Expectations Phase

Prior to and in the first days or hours of an experience, participants will have clear expectations of what the experience will be like as well as a sense of their hopes and fears stemming from the experience.

2. Exposure Phase

The first hours or days in the experience will be the exposure phase where the sights, sounds, smells, faces, names and some narratives will populate their

initial experience. For some this can be an exciting phase while for others it can be quite daunting. Many students, especially if the experience is quite novel or to some extent risqué, may experience a honeymoon element within the exposure phase; a time of adventure and feel-good altruism.

3. Reframing Phase

The exposure phase will give way to the reframing phase whereby the elements of expectation or stereotypes already planted in the participant's Semantic Memory are rearranged and reframed to fit the reality. This period within an experience is a critical time for program mentors to be proactively engaged with participants in assisting them to make sense of their experience through the lens of the program concepts and content.

4. Disillusionment Phase

Most participants will at some point go through a disillusionment phase where the excitement may give way to the humdrum of the everyday, even within a quite different experience. Participants may experience negative trigger events that clash with prior expectations. Culture shock, prior prejudice or stereotypes may be hooked by some event or simply the 'glamour' has worn off. This is a vital time for reflection upon experience to both continue and go deeper.

5. Awareness Phase

Fairly quickly, and especially if assisted by the active involvement of program mentors, participants will begin to grow in deeper awareness. During this period the program concepts and content begin to make sense and have a 'face' and a context. Participants' communication skills are beginning to grow, initial fears have been transcended, and a degree of comfort is now beginning to be established within the experience. This is an important time for social analysis and theological reflection as the participant now has a lot more data to work with and reframe from.

6. Agency Phase

Finally participants will begin to emerge into the agency phase where they have a real sense that they can and are making a difference. Hopefully they will be growing to a depth of awareness that the difference they are making is reciprocated by those they are in relationship with. The program concepts and content have now framed the experience so that the participants are beginning to truly and more deeply understand what the experience is really about.

Importance of time

The time element is very important for the effectiveness of any heightened experience in meeting the goals of the program. In general, the longer the time the participant is engaged in the experience and is reflecting upon their experience, the more effective the program will be. While a high quality, conceptually informed and well debriefed one-off experience may be beneficial in general, longer experiences do provide a much more holistic educational context for transformation and worldview change.

Potential dangers – short term or one-off experiences

The potential dangers of a one off, short term Service Learning experience include:

a. lack of time to unpack a negative event experienced during the service

b. lack of time to build a more 'real' relationship with the 'clients' of the service (personalisation)

c. the danger that the participant only experiences either a honeymoon or negative experience both divorced from reality

d. possible reinforcement of prior stereotypes

e. possible reinforcement of prejudice

f. shallow or non-learning

g. lip service to the value of the experience

h. shallow analysis of the situation

i. emotional disequilibrium

j. lack of time to build social and communication skills, and thus build confidence.

Psychological processes

As participants journey through the various phases and reflect upon their experience, they experience particular psychological processes. It is important that program mentors be aware of these if they are to best enable participants to get the most out of their experience and for true learning to occur.

Cognitive and Emotional Dissonance

Cognitive Dissonance is when an aspect of the experience clashes with a preconceived image, expectation or belief held in the student's Semantic Memory.

It sort of surprised me because a lot of them had sort of mobile phones and stuff, Walkmans and stuff and I did not think they would have anything like that at all. Yeah – some of them were really nice – none of them were actually really rude at all. There were a couple that were mumbling and stuff but I'm sure they had their reasons.

Journal reflection from Noel on Eddie's Van.

The example cited above under Emotional Dissonance could also be linked to the psychological processes associated with shock. Any strong emotional response within the service context has both the potential for learning and the potential for harm. One can never underestimate the value and role of the mentor in assisting the learning process and helping our young people negotiate these vital learning opportunities.

Emotional Dissonance is when the student has a strong and unexpected (often negative) response to an event at the service site that draws them out of their comfort zone. This event may clash with a prior 'honeymoon' image linked to the service experience.

> A student new to volunteering on the hospitality van was serving eggs from the BBQ when a homeless man in the line verbally abused him for giving him a "runny egg". The young person was quite shaken by what was said to him and how. After approaching the homeless man and challenging him gently about his abuse the supervising teacher took the student aside to see how they were. Over the coming days the teacher engaged with the student, inviting them into personal reflection and reframing linked to the incident. The student was able to frame the incident, after the initial emotional dissonance, in terms of mental illness.

Shock and Guilt

> **Shock: a sharp emotional and psychological jolt to a student's perception of reality within the service experience.**

> Early one morning at the Breakfast van associated with the homeless a fight broke out between four of the younger homeless men. The fight seemed to come out of nowhere. Beforehand the atmosphere at the van was warm and welcoming with the food being served and conversations shared. Students were catching up with homeless people they knew by name and checking in with them. The fight got quite physical to the point where the mentors (supervisors) felt the need to call a 'now' situation whereby the BBQ was quickly closed and the students returned to school. The incident was the prime focus for a debrief upon arrival at school. For some students, the incident broke them out of a honeymoon period associated with the van.

Guilt can be a wonderful entry point to a deeper social analysis, to a critique of one's worldview and insight into the dynamics of the relationship the student has with the other within the experience. We are seeking respectful, reciprocal relationships built upon empathy and empowerment.

Guilt can often be a natural response as the clients of the service program become real people with narratives, personal characteristics and circumstances. As the student grows in a sense of their worldview, and the power and privilege present in their own lives, they can feel overly responsible for or a need to be responsive to the situations of powerlessness and poverty they encounter.

> The Year 9 students from a school were regularly visiting a nursing home as a heightened experience within the Service Learning program. In the briefing the concepts of 'coming as guest', 'being deeply present', the value of story and wasting time with another, were introduced and unpacked. One young woman grew quite

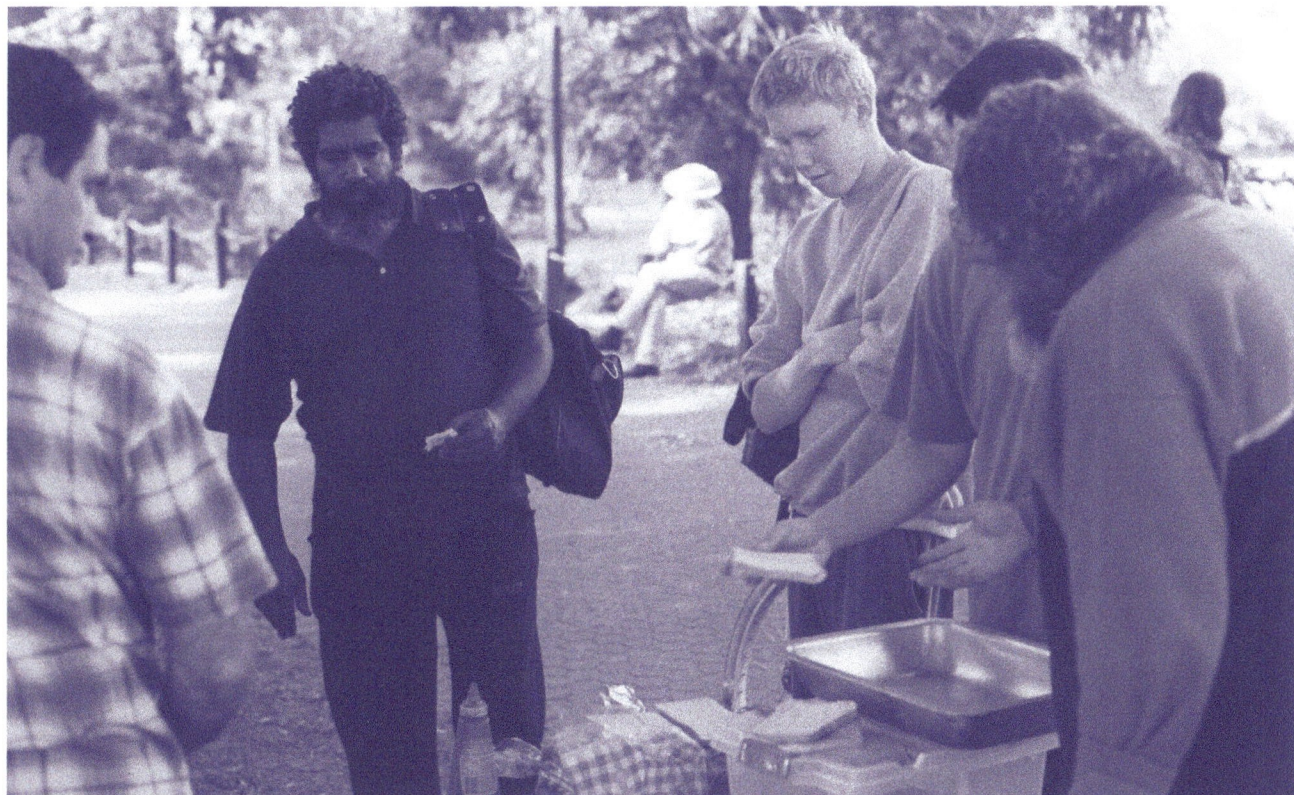

attached to an elderly gentleman who had fought in the Korean War. The man received few visitors and was always alone when the student arrived. Each time the student left she felt guilty that she was going home to a warm and welcoming environment and leaving him all alone. When the program came to a conclusion the girl felt quite guilty and powerless as she said farewell for the last time. The nursing home was on the other side of the city and continuing the visits was quite impractical. The program mentors spent time with her, helping her to reflect on her experience and to grow in the awareness that all relationships, no matter how good, have their limits.

Sometimes the emotional dissonance and shock is linked to a trigger event. The Service Learning practitioner welcomes the trigger event as it can provide natural and deep material for reflection and insight.

Trigger Events

> A trigger event is an event in which the student is confronted with another's circumstance or behaviour to some significant extent beyond the typical day-to-day dynamics of the experience. It is normally 'one off', bounded by time and circumstance, but creates emotional and cognitive dissonance.

The trigger event may well be positive. Every heightened experience will have its own unique trigger events and each is a potentially significant learning window. The trigger event creates a cognitive disequilibrium: a comfort or discomfort or confusion brought about by new information that must either be assimilated or accommodated into one's cognitive structure.

Trigger events point to the importance of reflection upon experience. If we are not careful they can occur, pass us by and no learning occurs.

If reflected upon, the trigger event can stimulate deeper awareness within the student of both their own life situation and the complex sociological context they are engaging with. The power of the trigger event is that it is natural, coming from within the experience, and causes immediate emotional and cognitive disequilibrium.

> In one situation a student had been visiting the elderly in a nursing home most Mondays for a whole term. One elderly gentleman whom the student had spent time with each

week did not appear to be very responsive. What stories that were shared were often repeated and many times the gentleman was asleep for much of the visit. At times, despite the heightened experience being framed with concepts such as 'guest', 'presence' and 'dignity' the student was unsure of the value of the experience. One Monday, as the student was about to leave, the elderly man simply said, "Nick, I really look forward to your visits – thank you!"

This experience would be a good example of a trigger event that led to much food for reflection and insight.

Epiphany – light bulb moments

> **Light Bulb moment: a moment of awareness or insight often linked to deeper meaning-making.**

Experiences such as Nick's encounter with the elderly nursing home resident, or the reframing through reflection of the egg incident in terms of mental illness, can result in students having an epiphany, 'ah-ha' or 'light bulb' moment that leads to increased awareness. These moments may be very simple, as simple as a homeless man inviting students to come under a shelter when rain begins to fall, or an elderly person in a nursing home remembering the student's name or offering them a chair.

Conscious Awareness

> **Conscious Awareness is the deliberate choice (linked to associated skills) to expect, identify, become aware of and remain alert for aspects of the experience that will populate the experience beyond the norm. The openness and sensitivity associated with conscious awareness will provide a rich and ever-changing canvas which will lead to deeper meaning-making from the experience.**

The van has been great as it provided such a strong feeling of community. Also it feels good to help out people (though

sometimes I wonder who helps who) and I enjoy the feeling of acceptance that some homeless provide to us.

Journal Reflection from Adam on Eddie's Van.

I felt valued when I was getting along with a person, and was having a positive conversation with him smiling; he was asking me questions as well. He was laughing with me and he smiled and said goodbye and patted me on the back. They would wave to us when we were driving away. I felt like this because they were coming as a guest to me, and being open and friendly and making me feel accepted as well.

Journal Reflection from Colin on Eddie's Van.

In the journal reflections above, Adam comes to a point of conscious awareness of wondering "who helps who?" while Colin has grown to a point of awareness where he can see that the homeless have come as 'guest' to him!

Grappling

> Grappling is where the student actively and deliberately engages with the stimuli present at the service site. Grappling is the student dance between what has been introduced to their Semantic Memory and that which they are experiencing in their Episodic Memory. It is where the 'learning' in Service Learning occurs.

In grappling, the student is in the middle of meaning-making linked to the experience. In grappling the student may:

a. recall elements of curriculum

b. play with cause-and-effect modalities

c. allow social analysis questions to arise

d. make links to other stimuli

e. become aware of their feeling responses

and discuss or reflect upon all of these with other participants or program mentors. Grappling is a sifting of the experience in the context of the deliberately engaged-with values, concepts and language of the program. Grappling leads to either accommodation or assimilation.

Accommodation

> Accommodation is where the student, through grappling with new information linked to the experience, and with concepts introduced to their Semantic Memory, potentially changes or expands their worldview or experiences new learning about others, society or oneself.

In Adam and Colin's reflections above they have accommodated new learning into their worldview. They have now come to a point where the reciprocal nature of their service relationship with the homeless has become real, apparent and experienced by them. Colin now knows that while he has attempted to 'come as guest' to the homeless, they in turn have engaged in that same respect-filled way with him.

Assimilation

> Assimilation is where new information is made to fit one's existing worldview, stereotypes and beliefs – potentially precluding learning.

In contrast other students may have sought to assimilate the event. Through accommodation students will begin to revise their stereotypical ideas and develop them into more open, complex, and accurate concepts. Accommodation is a more in-depth cognitive process associated with a deeper level of and more complex understanding of the dynamics of the experience and society in general.

> *The things that confuse me are the reasons that some of the people are on the streets and how come they can't just reconnect with their loved ones and leave the streets?*
>
> Journal Reflection from Terry on Eddie's Van.

Personalisation

> Personalisation is the process whereby the people you are relating to go beyond labels and stereotypes to be people you know by name. You know some of their story and your relationship is real and personal.

> *I think they think of us as friends, people they can joke around with, and like with the guy that always taps people on the shoulder – Trevor. He is always tapping you on the shoulder and you always know that it is him and he always points to someone – and you always play along with it – and it is just good fun and other times you will just go up to someone and you will have a very light-hearted chat and it really gives a sense of friendship, kind of getting along with them, friendly, a bit of fun.*
>
> Journal Reflection from James on Eddie's Van.

Divided Self

> The 'Divided self' is a term used to label the process whereby a participant feels conflicted between their experience at the service site and their values, beliefs, understandings and worldview formed by their family of origin and life experiences prior to service.

> *What still confuses me is when some of them buy alcohol and drugs, why don't they be stricter on themselves so they can try to break the cycle of homelessness?*
>
> Journal reflection by Matthew on Eddie's Van.

Normalisation

> Normalisation is the process where the important contextual presenting data that frames an experience and is originally

> foreign to the student has now faded from conscious awareness. The unkempt homeless man, the adolescent sleeping rough, the lonely nursing home resident that had originally claimed the attention of the student is now just part of the scene and no longer drawing any specific attention. These aspects of the service site are now 'normal' and not claiming attention.

A group of students were on an immersion in South Africa. Driving from Johannesburg airport the students were aghast at the poverty they were witnessing in the shanty towns. The litter, raw sewage, roaming dogs, children playing in squalor, all shocked the students on the immersion. Less than ten days later as the group travelled from one immersion situation to another the same squalor outside the bus window had become normal and accepted as the same students checked in by texting with friends back in Australia. What had originally shocked them had quickly faded into the background and under the 'awareness bar'.

In normalisation, the awareness bar has been lowered. In so doing the danger is that important stimuli and aspects of the experience are not attended to, not focussed upon as the student is not even aware of them anymore.

By continually reflecting upon experience, and by creative approaches to keeping the awareness bar high, the mentor mitigates against the effects of normalisation. Simple initiatives that will help the student maintain conscious awareness linked to experience, and invite the student to deeper analysis, include:

- providing students with new sets of reflection questions
- assigning students new tasks within the experience
- inviting students to focus on particular elements of the now familiar experience (e.g., focusing on the names of the clients)
- inviting students to deeper levels of reflection upon their experience
- inviting students to identify concepts gained from their experience and apply these to other aspects of their lives.

Conscious Awareness of Unjust Structures

> Conceptual Normalisation: On the Meta or conceptual level there is a danger that those coming from a place of privilege can normalise injustice and poverty.

Without continual reflection upon experience and the active presence of mentors, not only will the presenting day to day data from the service site become normal and fade into the background, this same process may also apply to bigger and structural awarenesses. The student in normalising the situation, may normalise the poverty or disadvantage and refrain from thinking critically about it and its associated unjust structures. We call this 'conceptual normalisation'. This lack of critical thinking may:

- deepen patronising attitudes
- lead to a cognitive assimilation whereby there is little or no change in service learner attitudes and prejudice
- maintain or even reinforce stereotypes.

Conceptual Normalisation may lead to a student thinking that it is acceptable for people to be living on the streets, for people to be trapped in poverty in a majority world slum, for asylum seekers to be trapped in detention centres, or for the elderly not to be receiving quality care and attention in a nursing home.

The program mentor's role is to assist the student to accommodate their new experiences into an expanded worldview through critical reflection. Students now become engaged in the learning process, asking causal questions about the 'why' and 'how' of the poverty of people they now are in relationship with.

Worldview

> **Worldview: the personal and conceptual map of the world from which one derives meaning and understanding.**

In any heightened service experience there will be, to varying degrees, dissonance and values clashes with the student's already existing worldview.

Accordion Effect

> **Accordion Effect: an expansion or stretching of one's worldview leading to deeper causal analysis, a broader understanding of concepts, and a holistic appreciation of the nature and meaning of an experience.**

Through processes of confirmation and disconfirmation, reflection and analysis the goal of the Service Learning program will be to expand, change or modify the student's worldview and thus contribute to the bringing about of the reign of God.

Disconfirmation and Confirmation

> **Confirmation and disconfirmation: confirming or not confirming the connections between student experience (Episodic Memory) and expectation (held in Semantic Memory) and engaging in the interplay between active and anticipatory cognition.**

Both confirmation and disconfirmation can be opportunities for learning. Sometimes participants will assimilate their emotional and cognitive responses to their experience into prior mind-maps and continue on in the experience with little or no learning occurring. Sometimes, faced with disconfirmation, learners can revise the models of meaning and expectations that they use to construct

their Service Learning experience and thereby modify the very cognitive affective representations that they use to structure, make meaning of, and pre-shape their world. In other words, accommodation has occurred and the accordion effect is operating.

The goal of an effective Service Learning program is to deliberately inform Semantic Memory with our core concepts, plan for relevant experiences that engage these concepts, and then creatively reflect on the student experience. When this occurs the student's experience with go beyond normalisation and personalisation to an expanded worldview. The accordion effect will thus lead to more accommodated learning and a more just world for all.

Eddie's Van is a very rewarding experience and it is integral to our duties as Catholics in society today. I am glad that I participate in the program because not only has it taught me a lot more about homelessness in Australia today but it also makes me feel that I am taking action on my beliefs. Too often in society today we talk about ending poverty and helping the poor but don't take action, and by doing Eddie's Van I feel that I am acting on my beliefs and putting words into action. I believe Eddie's Van is core to Gregory Terrace as a Catholic Edmund Rice school because we are taught that we should help the poor and we say that we have a duty to follow Jesus' teachings, but unless we do something such as the van we are not putting the beliefs we have into action.

Journal reflection from Adam on Eddie's Van.

Reflection is the key to learning

An effective Service Learning program may provide the significant by-product of increasing the students' reflection and analysis skills. Sadly in the twenty-first century, reflection is not easy nor popular with many youth. However reflection can be taught and in time students come to see its purpose, especially if there is an authenticity about it and an obvious value.

While service is core to any school that is based on the Gospel, the experience of service in itself is not necessarily educational or 'life changing'. The power of Service Learning lies in the reflection engaged in, prior to and after the service experience, through the lens of the core values of the community.

It is not enough for members of the community to just experience the core values of the community. It is when community members engage with the core values, experience them directly or indirectly in curriculum and culture, and then reflect upon this experience, that the values grow in Semantic Memory and becomes personally owned.

As always, reflection upon experience must be user friendly. It will also take a multitude of forms.

Sometimes the reflection is powerful and overt. At other times it is subtle and indirect. But the rhythm is the same – **Semantic Memory – Episodic Memory – Reflection – personal ownership** – as Semantic Memory stretches and deepens and the accordion effect comes into play.

Reflection

Reflection upon experience takes a myriad of forms. Reflection will vary depending upon the type of experience that we are engaging in, the audience, the sought-after outcomes from the learning experience, our skill set and student need.

Reflection creates and allows space for meaning-making to occur, allows space for the dots to be joined, for the Semantic Memory to link A with B – concepts held often tentatively in Semantic Memory.

Reflection may:

- Stand back from the experience in order to identify patterns.

- Allow particular stimuli to come to the fore in being stronger and more significant.

- Allow a question, a deeper question, to surface from within the experience.

- Allow the unseen face to come to the fore, the hidden surface – for the background to come to the foreground.
- Allow the participant to select a conceptual 'coat hanger' to associate with a particular element of the experience.
- Engage particular language from the theology and spirituality of the community as a means for going to deeper insight and meaning.

Reflection leads to:

a. the forming of associations
b. the raising of images
c. deeper understanding of concepts
d. the breaking down of prior understanding or stereotypes
e. broader contexts to be mapped, and more.

Reflection will often lead to an 'ah ha' moment, a light bulb moment where Semantic Memory goes "Yes!" as it sees a link, goes deeper, forms associations, and now understands. What is core is the ability of the learning space to flexibly engage with stimuli which will harness the energy already at work in the interplay. This is the dance between a participant's experiences held in Episodic Memory, and what has deliberately been introduced into Semantic Memory.

Reflection will:

a. mirror the skill set of the teacher
b. not seek to manipulate the outcome
c. provide as wide a variety of forms of reflection as possible to respond to student need and learning style.

During the course of a quality Service Learning program the student may have the following experiences. Throughout each of them we will hopefully hook or engage every student's way of making sense, of learning, and of finding meaning from experience. The students experiences may include:

- silence
- role play
- ritual
- open-ended questions
- simulation games
- focused writing

- guest speakers
- symbolism
- audio-visuals
- music
- sacred text
- physical movement (drama).

Experience therefore sometimes plays the dual role of being both the vehicle in Episodic Memory through which the student experiences the content or concept, AND the way of reflecting upon the experience itself.

On one occasion students had been working with the students from a Special School for two weeks as part of a Rich task in Year 10. On the second last night of the 'immersion' a retreat was held to reflect on the students' experience of their encounters. A large candle was in the centre of a darkened room. The students were invited to come forward and pick up a candle in a foil cup, and a card. The students wrote the first name of the student they had most interacted with on one side of the card and wrote a short letter to them on the other side thanking them for the privilege of the time shared. When all was completed the students were invited to come forward one by one, light the candle and form a circle 'holding' the sacred story of the person they had built relationship with. The song Holy Ground by John Michael Talbot was played. The ritual concluded with the students naming out loud the first name of the person they had 'encountered' – for example "David" – and then placing the card (letter) and candle around the Christ candle – before forming an arms linked tighter circle.

This ritual was powerful and was identified by many participants as one of the highlights of the service experience. In this ritual the concept of 'innate dignity' that had been a focus of their interactions was again 'experienced' through the closing ritual. The students were 'reflecting' or engaging simply through their experience of a meaningful ritual.

Reflection in practice

Eddie's Morning Breakfast Van

St Joseph's College, Gregory Terrace has for many years had a hospitality van linked to the homeless community of inner-city Brisbane as part of their school culture and Service Learning program. Eddie's Van and its associated values and concepts have become part of the culture of the community. This Service Learning heightened experience involving Eddie's Van took the form of:

- interaction between the students and the homeless at the BBQ site
- serving breakfast and night snacks
- practical tasks of setting up and cleaning up.

After a morning of chatting with the homeless in an inner-city park and serving breakfast, the first level of reflection would take place. While driving back to school in the minibus the teacher would ask the students, "What was something significant during your morning and why?" Or it may have been, "If you could think of a word or words that sum up your morning what would they be and why?"

The conversation that flowed was simple but often profound. After the clean-up back at school the students would spend about five minutes filling in a page of their SL journal:

a. What was the highlight of your experience and why?

b. What was difficult and why?

c. Any other comments and why?

This journaling time was very short, but deliberate and sacred. After every second time that the students experienced their encounter with the homeless there was a facilitated conversation held in class about the experience; a conversation wrapped around key reflective questions.

So the students had the core concepts associated with this 'Service Learning' introduced to them and broken open in the classroom (Semantic Memory), had their experience of engaging deliberately and reflectively with the homeless at the hospitality van (Episodic Memory), and then undertook three varying types of reflection upon their experience within ten days of the experience taking place. Over time, and through the reflection upon their experience, key concepts grew in the students' understanding and gradually became a part of their lens (or worldview). A series of simple reflection techniques linked to experience form Chapter 5 of this guide. While these techniques are valuable, the most valuable are those that come from the teacher or mentors' own skill and experience set.

Timing of reflection

It is important for reflection upon experience to be positioned as close as possible to the actual experience. This ensures that the feelings linked to the experience are captured along with faces, names, stories and reactions. There is great value in this. Program mentors will also note when a student has had a 'bad' experience at the service site and consequently ensure they are followed up in some way later in the day. There is also value in other reflective spaces further distanced from the experience itself. This allows time for the experience itself to sit, and to be mulled over in Semantic Memory linked to concepts deliberately engaged there. It also allows time for participants to gain perspective, and for informal discussions to take place.

Reflection process

The basic structure or flow of the reflection process is:

a. Core concepts linked to the values of the community are identified.

b. These concepts are deliberately engaged in as a result of the planning of the relevant normative or heightened experiences.

c. The concepts are introduced into the Semantic Memory of the student and contextualised by their particular experiences. In some cases the concepts are embedded into the formal curriculum with links to the experience. In other cases informally embedded within the culture of the community. In other cases they are particularised through the experiences of the student in the Service Learning program.

d. In the briefing, the concepts are revisited through processes linked to:

- conscious awareness
- attention to stimuli
- focus questions
- cause and effect modalities
- cognitive and emotional dissonance
- anticipatory cognition and active cognition
- social analysis skills
- theological reflection skills, and
- stimulation and arousal of Episodic Memory.

e. During 'grappling' – the process whereby the student actively and deliberately engages with the stimuli present at the service site – students will:

- focus on particular stimuli
- recall program concepts and values
- recall program ideology and language
- place a pertinent reflective or social analysis question into their Semantic Memory and then engage with it
- recall relevant elements of the curriculum
- make links to other stimuli
- become aware of their response to feeling, and
- deliberately engage with the theology of the program and use the language and concepts of Gospel Service engagement to focus their engagement with the 'other'.

f. The processes associated with grappling continue beyond the experience itself and into debriefing, exit and closure processes.

It will be during, or because of the reflection upon experience through the lens of the core values and associated concepts, that the learning in Service Learning will occur. This learning will parallel the meaning-making journey of the student. With the assistance of program mentors, students will go from surface to deeper meaning-making and possibly to a profound personal worldview change.

CHAPTER 4
Living into a Culture of Encounter

This is a while back. I was talking to a guy named Richard and he is a guy who comes and is always complaining about something; the food is not cooked or something or the serving is too slow or something. And I said to myself, "Nah, fair enough, he has got something wrong with him or something, [a] don't go there kind of thing." And he is talking about how the guy owes him some money and if he does not pay this guy he will be kicked out of his rental and so he needs the money owed to him real bad, he has been trying to get this money for a while. And he was talking about drugs and all of this and I kind of felt, I was tempted to think, "Hey, you've got yourself into this situation!" But I did not go there, I just sat there and listened, listened to his story and was kind of there for him.

Journal reflection from Paul on Eddie's Van.

Finding meaning

One of our primary motivations for engaging in Service Learning is to create situations and experiences where young people can have their worldview modified or changed. Another prime motivation is to help our young people experience the core values of our communities in a real and authentic way. In all of this we hope that this 'culture of encounter' will make a lasting impression on our young people's hearts. If the young person finds meaning and purpose through our service learning, then we have taken a significant step towards assisting them to experience true inner liberation.

Alison Le Cornu

Alison Le Cornu from the University of Surrey in the United Kingdom has discovered much about the journey of internalisation and meaning-making linked to experience. Le Cornu identified four levels of meaning-making.

Le Cornu identified that some people within an experiential situation would remain at a 'surface' or information level of internalisation or meaning-making. Often these people remained locked in prior stereotypical thinking, or situations of non-learning or even reinforced bias. Most however would progress past the surface meaning-making to deeper internalisation of what they were experiencing.

Surface

When working with students engaged with the homeless, a small number of students remained locked in reflecting that the homeless were good blokes who made them welcome. They would think that their (the students') role was to barbecue some food for them and offer them a cup of coffee. The meaning-making remained at the surface level.

Deeper

Others went to a much deeper level of meaning-making. Some students began to use words such as 'community', 'their home', 'their turf', 'acceptance', 'mutual', and 'reciprocal'. Most students began to articulate quite deep and sophisticated levels of meaning linked to their experience.

Tacit

Over time, levels of meaning-making will continue to change if reflection upon experience in the context of our core values and concepts continues. Some through an experience will progress their meaning-making from

deeper to tacit. Tacit is where a student continues to reflect upon their experiences and associated 'deeper' meaning-making concepts and language. As this is done, the meaning-making energy is released to seek out even deeper levels of meaning. The initial deeper levels of meaning-making have become tacit, expected, assumed.

> Tacit meaning-making is where profound encounters take place. If, for example, a student reflects that when they engage with refugee or asylum seeker youth they feel welcomed and accepted, then they will find meaning in the encounter. If that same student continues to reflect on the dynamics of their encounters, then after some time they begin to 'expect' welcome and acceptance. This expecting can be a real Kairos moment when the meaning-making energy, now freed up, is ready for deeper levels of meaning. Through reflection they can become aware of reciprocity or trauma in the other's narrative, or facets of personal freedom that they had never envisaged. This is the energy of Tacit meaning-making.

Existential change

Some students within an experience will come to quite profound levels of meaning-making. In these levels their meaning-making will reflect a deep internalisation of the meaning-making process and the concepts and core values linked to their experience. This supports Le Cornu's understanding of existential change (Price, 2008, p. 313).

What makes for deeper meaning?

It is through their Service Learning experience that students may discover deeper levels of meaning leading to worldview modification or change. The following factors appear to be key in assisting this to happen:

a. time of volunteering and of building relationship
b. the active presence of program mentors
c. direct experience
d. program theology and spirituality
e. reflection upon experience
f. social analysis and critical thinking.

Time associated with volunteering

While time of itself does not necessarily point to a deeper level of meaning-making, it is nevertheless an influencing factor. More time building relationships with the people at a service site means that:

1. deeper relationships are built (personalisation)
2. trigger events are deepened and mined for real meaning and significance
3. cause and effect analysis is more holistic
4. there is time to go past both the honeymoon and the disillusionment phases of experience
5. communication skills are more highly developed, and
6. the theology and spirituality of the program has time to filter through their experiences and become more real and contextualised.

The active presence of program mentors

As in all learning settings the teacher or program mentor is not an idle spectator, but is actively engaged with the student within the experience. The mentor actively engaged with the student can focus attention on particular stimuli, ask pertinent questions that lead to deeper analysis, aid in increased awareness, ask open-ended questions that enable deeper lateral thinking, invite deeper reflection on trigger events and generally walk beside the student during their meaning-making journey.

Direct experience

A significant assistance to deeper meaning-making and a more profound experience for participants occurs when they are in direct relationship with the focus of the program; with the asylum seekers, with the homeless, with the land, with the elderly etc. Direct experience greatly enhances both the process of personalisation and the experience of the culture of the encounter.

Program theology/spirituality & relevant curriculum content

One significant factor that assists ever deeper levels of meaning-making is the ability of students to proactively explore the theology and spirituality of the program in their journaling and other forms of reflection on their experience. When the language of the supporting community's core values begins to appear in their day-to-day interactions and reflections it not only frames the students' experiences and allows for deeper analysis, but it is also a ladder to deeper meaning. This is because the theological or spirituality informed concepts in themselves go to the heart of why we do what we do.

Authentic and relevant curriculum content linked to the experience will also go a long way in assisting in deeper meaning-making.

Reflection upon experience

Theorists in the Service Learning field point to the importance of reflection upon experience. Some would claim that the youth of today do not naturally reflect in their fast paced multimedia over stimulated world. However, while some students will initially struggle with reflection, the authenticity of the experience will often motivate them to see its value and worth.

As we stated previously, reflection upon experience must be user friendly, meet student needs, be relevant to the particular experience, and become an integral part of the totality of the experience.

Social Analysis and Critical Thinking

The final factor that leads to students engaging in deeper meaning-making is the ability to engage

in social analysis and critical thinking. One of the great advantages of Service Learning is that it both engages personally with issues that idealistic youth are concerned with, while at the same time inviting critical thinking about those same issues.

Some of the key skills and approaches that lead to effective social analysis and critical thinking are:

1. search and research skills

2. awareness and observation skills

3. information to help filter findings, and

4. 'coat hangers' that assist in identifying relevant and causal factors.

Armed with these skills and youthful passion, students readily participate in experiences that they believe will make a difference. It is important in this dynamic that the program mentor is not telling the student what to think but rather inviting them to step out on a journey of discovery, in fact both self-discovery, and discovery that will enhance the society in which they live.

CHAPTER 5
Reflection and Engagement Techniques for the Practitioner

This chapter introduces some reflection and engagement techniques that Service Learning programs have used. Many of the ideas reflect the author's skill set and context. However, while some reflection techniques are outlined below, the best technique is that which comes from the professional mentor's own skill set and experience and is linked to student need.

1. Feeling techniques

1.1 Have a large variety of *feeling words* at the back of the student journal as a guide for them to place words upon what they are experiencing.

1.2 Have selective *feeling words on large A3 sheets* of paper on the ground and ask students, after reflecting for some minutes, to go and stand next to the 'feeling' that is most prominent for them from their experience. Then instruct students to journal about this for some minutes. Repeat this exercise three times.

1.3 As part of the in-class briefing time teach the students a process of **sitting by the door** of feelings. If, for example, the dominant feeling is FEAR, invite the student to write that down and then to sit with that feeling (along with the list of other feeling words described in 1.1). After some time, by sitting by the door of 'fear', other feelings 'behind the door' will surface, and typically these will be the reasons for their fear. For example: "I am feeling fear because I am uncertain about what to do or say!" Another feeling might be uncertainty. For this, sit by the door of uncertainty for some time, perhaps on the other side of that door will be "I don't feel that I have anything worthwhile saying, I should not be here … " There may be many different feelings. Insecurity, for another example! This process of sitting by the door can go for some time until the person feels that they have come to their primal feeling.

1.4 Place a whole series of **Photo Language** on the floor. Invite students to take their time and move around until they find one or two images that best relate to what they are feeling about the experience. After they select several images, instruct students to journal for a short time about why they chose that image. This could be followed up by sharing with another participant or with the whole group.

1.5 An alternative version of 1.4 is for students to take their own photos (away from the experience) or from magazines etc. that reflect their feelings. In so doing they are creating their own photo language.

2. Movement and drama

2.1 Play a **game of clumps** where you simply encourage students to just 'mill around' until you call out a number – and then the students must rush to form a clump with other students to make up that number. By doing so some are excluded and are put to the side. Keep playing until only about four students are left. Debrief by using concepts such as exclusion, 'in-groups' and 'out-groups', and acceptance. Ask a question like: "At the site working with the homeless – who appears to you not to be in the 'in-group'? Why do you think this may be the case?"

2.2 Place students into groups of five. Each student takes it in turn to **sculpt** the group into a freeze sculpture that reflects how they feel at the service site, or their analysis of what is going on at the service site. After the group have 'frozen', the student then reforms the other groups into a circle and explains their freeze sculpture to them. For example, "I placed Sarah facing outwards because …"

2.3 Have two balls of **coloured wool**. Form the students into a large circle. One student holds the end of one ball of wool and throws the rest of the ball to another student. While doing this the thrower names a 'gift' that that student (the catcher) brings to the group. The catcher then holds the wool and throws the rest of the ball to another student in the circle (who has not received the wool yet) and names their gift. While this is happening, the second ball of wool is released in the same fashion as the first. After some time there is a complex web of wool between the students filling the circle. As the facilitator, then use this image to talk about interconnectedness and interdependence as two key concepts, especially in Eco-spirituality experiences.

2.4 **Continuums:** As the facilitator, link a series of key questions to the experience. Do this within a structure of having the students stand around in the middle of the room. Let one end of the room represent one pole of response, the other end of the room a different pole. The facilitator may make a statement like, "I felt really comfortable at the service site today?" After hearing the statement the students respond by moving and standing at the pole that represents their response to the statement, or somewhere in between – from very comfortable to very uncomfortable. After each question you may ask two or three students to explain why they are standing where they are. Repeat this activity with five or six more statements that have a polarity factor associated with them.

2.5 **Shoe throw:** Invite the students to form a circle. Invite each student to throw one of their shoes into the middle of the room. The facilitator (yourself or an assistant) then picks up one shoe and pretends to attempt to put it onto their foot. The facilitator then reminds the group of the falsity of the statement, "Walk in the shoes of your brother or sister for a mile!" You can never truly walk in another's shoes. This simple activity is ideal for breaking open the concept of 'guest'. It can then be used to move on to the sacred story of the other as a guest. The imagery can be powerful.

3. Cause and effect – social analysis

3.1 Have a **small jigsaw puzzle**. Spread the pieces out over a large table. Gather the students around the table and say, "You have five minutes to put the jigsaw puzzle together!" (Don't show the students the picture of the puzzle). Hopefully there will be frenzied activity as the students find small pieces with red on them that end up being part of a truck etc. When the five minutes is up – invite the students to reflect on the exercise. Obviously they will be a little frustrated.

Then, as either teacher or mentor, spend time elaborating on how they have been working with refugees now (for example) for four days or with the homeless people for three days. Ask, "Do you think that after four days you understand the world of a refugee or homeless person?" The concept here is that homelessness is a complex issue, and it is unreasonable to expect that after only a couple of hours of working with homeless people some students can think they know what homelessness is like. This can be a great exercise when taking students on an immersion.

3.2 In following up on 3.1 a good exercise is to have a whole series of **'blank' jigsaw puzzle pieces**. Each day during reflection time the students can be asked, "What pieces of the jigsaw puzzle (which they are to imagine represents life in a Special School) do you THINK you may have picked up today and why?" The students then write their 'insights' on the jigsaw pieces. This can be done each day during an experience. By the end of the experience (e.g., an immersion) students will have come to a real understanding of the complexities of any service sub-culture and hence the importance of not rushing to conclusions. The blank jigsaw puzzle pieces that they do manage to identify may lead to some cause and effect associations. The teacher or mentor will caution against reading too much into these associations given the limited time and experience the student has had.

3.3 Within a focus on the concept of cause and effect, invite students after some time into their experience to identify the **'elements' – the 'causal' elements** – that go to making up the total context they are engaging with. If the group identify eight elements on the first reflection time, then another six the following time and then seven more on the third – you can then (as a creative example) populate a large sheet of butcher's paper with the 21 'elements' that appear to map the causal factors associated with that 'issue'. Then type these up on an A4 sheet. Invite the students – working in groups – to draw 'effect' lines between the various elements identified. When completed, invite the students to reflect on what they see, perhaps suggesting concepts such as, "Several elements are linked to more than one other element." Or, "Element X appears to have a lot of lines drawn to it!" If this same activity is repeated using a separate issue from the students' own life experiences (e.g., bullying at school or acceptance at school), follow up by comparing their answers to the latter question to their answers to their original reflections. In doing so the cause-and-effect concept will grow deeply within the Semantic Memory of the students.

3.4 Play **a simulation game** with the students, focusing on an issue of Social Justice. Ideally the game would involve some of the issues and concepts they are engaging with through their Service Learning experience. By playing a simulation game before developing their own, students are becoming familiar with the 'game format' and the stencil they will use for their own creativity. Then identify a core format for the game (e.g., a continuum or circle movement). Instruct the students then to either select a character they have met, or which they think they may meet through their experience, and then identify seven or eight life events that may happen to that character – assigning each event a positive or negative score according to whether the event leads to a higher quality of life or takes from it. After spending time discussing their characters with other students, instruct the group to then play the simulation game. The ideal game is one that leads to students physically moving 'up' or 'down' the continuum, or in towards the centre of the circle, or out away from 'belonging' or 'acceptance' or other key concepts. After playing the game the group reflects on their experience of it, and any insights they received. Another facet of this idea may be to swap games with other groups that have come up with their own game.

3.5 On the internet or wherever you would like to source them, locate a series of cartoons associated with various Social Justice Issues of the day. Invite the students to reflect on the cartoons. Then – after discussion of the cartoons – see if the group has any amateur illustrators/artists among them: ask them to draw their own cartoon with the salient features of the justice experience they are engaging with highlighted. This can be a great catalyst for discussion.

3.6 **Wool Tie:** Especially if the service involves an issue of strong social injustice, invite students to write on cards the elements or context of the situation that contributes to the social injustice. Then invite a student (or approach a student beforehand and invite them to volunteer) to sit on a chair in the middle of the room. The student is then blindfolded. Stress in words how serious this 'role play' is. Then indicate that the volunteer now symbolises everyone who is trapped in an unjust situation (e.g., a refugee, a homeless person etc). In a room of silence, encourage the students one by one to come out and read what they have written or their cards, then loosely tie some wool around the volunteer – tying them to the chair (around the torso, the legs, the arms etc). There may be a giggle or two at first – mainly out of nervousness – but then the atmosphere will quickly become serious. After all the elements on the cards are named and the person is very well tied down, you will then have a scene that powerfully shows how poverty in its many forms entraps. You may then ask the volunteer how they 'felt' as they were tied down.

A debrief of this activity is especially important. So when ready, use a pair of scissors to cut one of the wool ties and either name a good quality that the volunteer has OR suggest ways of breaking the bonds of injustice. This continues until the volunteer is totally freed.

4. Audio visual/other stimulus

4.1 Show a **film or documentary** that engages with the particular service experience. The context of the experience within the curriculum will determine how long or pivotal the film and the reflection upon experience will be. An example might be the 2004 Australian film 'Tom White' staring Colin Friels which breaks open causal factors leading to homelessness. It is important that any such film is not just shown but rather briefed and debriefed through the lens of the core presenting concepts.

4.2 Invite students to engage with a large collection of **magazines or images** on the internet and present a PowerPoint or other presentation whereby the students associate particular images with their feeling responses – images that are linked to their service experience. Present each image in a folio along with fifty words for each image which demonstrate why that image speaks to their reflection on and insights gained from the experience.

4.3 Place a large menagerie of **objects and/or symbols** in the middle of the reflection space. Similar to the photo language activity, invite students to spend time circling the objects until they have found two or three that speak to their experience and meaning-making. Objects such as a watch or pen, a family photo or flower or sunglasses, may evoke a particular feeling linked to their meaning-making from the experience.

4.4 **Ritual and Symbol** can be powerful ways to deepen and focus reflection upon experience. In this activity Invite the students to sketch a significant person from their experience OR write that person's first name on a card. Play a reflective song such as Be Not Afraid (St Louis Jesuits) or St Therese's Prayer (John Michael Talbot) or You take My Breath Away (Eva Cassidy) and invite the students to form a large circle. Instruct the students to hold their card or drawing in their hands for some time – honouring the innate dignity of the person represented on their card or drawing. After this, instruct them to reverently place their drawing or card around a Christ Candle in the middle of the room, and pick up a T-light candle from the centre of the pile that is forming. After placing their card with the person's name or drawing, the student then 'holds' the candle (holds the person) in silence for some time. After a few minutes, at the facilitator's instruction the student places the T-light candle next to the name card or drawing, and reverently states the person's name. After each student carries out this activity, the ritual concludes with a blessing.

4.5 **Label game:** Invite eight students to come forward. Place a label onto their foreheads with words such as loser, leader, fragile, tough, shy, nice, lazy, stupid. The students who have volunteered do not know the words on their labels. The remainder of the students form a circle around the eight students in the 'role play'. The eight students now verbally engage with one another around a topic (e.g., "you are planning the Student Formal") but do so treating each other as if the label the others are wearing are true. Allow the role play to extend for about ten minutes. When debriefing the students ask:

- Did you become aware of what your label was? How?

- Did you enjoy your label?

- How did it feel to be labelled?

Once this debrief is concluded, ask the whole group to reflect on what labels they have experienced or used when engaging in their particular service activity or experience. This can lead to a very good discussion and reflection on experience.

4.6 **Card game:** Break the students into teams of six and give each team a pack of cards. Instruct them to deal out the cards evenly until there are none left. The object of the game is to get rid of your cards first. Any student can begin. They are to do so by placing a card out into the middle. Then the next student must place in the middle a higher card (going from 2 being the lowest to Ace then Joker being the highest). Suits do not matter. If the student cannot put out a higher card they must say "Pass". Once the students have gone around and no one can put out a higher card, then the person who put out the last card (the highest) has won that round. The cards in the middle are then placed to one side and the 'winner' begins again. This continues until one person has got rid of all of their cards; they are the 'winner' or King. The game goes on until the second person has no cards remaining – they are the Queen (or whatever 'power' term you wish to use). The game continues further until the last person is labelled 'the biggest loser' (with the second last being the 'loser'). The cards are then reshuffled, and the students sit in a circle from 1 (highest) to 6 (lowest). When the cards are re-dealt the 'biggest loser' gives their two best cards to the King and the King gives their two worst cards to the biggest loser. The 'Queen' and 'loser' exchange one card in a similar fashion. The game continues through another round in this vein. The game is NOT fair. It is very difficult for the biggest loser to progress up the scale. The game is about FEELINGS associated with power and powerlessness. Awareness of feelings is key. Once the game has progressed for about 30 minutes, stop the game and invite players to reflect on how they felt. Often the person who was King loves the role and the power and often the 'biggest loser' is frustrated. The vital element now is for the facilitator to then invite the students to reflect on the power dynamic within their service experience using the card game as a ladder to deeper reflection.

4.7 **Cards finger observation:** Purchase a set of jumbo cards (large playing cards). Select nine cards, possibly the 2, 3, 4, 5, 6, 7, 8, 9, 10 (the suit doesn't matter). Place the nine cards face up on the ground and gather the students around. Ask, "What do you see? How many are there?" Ask this while kneeling (or sitting) on the ground with your hands to either side of the cards – and with a certain number of your fingers unobtrusively touching the ground. Let students take turns guessing the answer to the apparently easy question of how many cards there are. Each time say '"No" to the students' answers unless their answer is the same as the number of fingers you have touching the ground. Shuffle the cards over and over and then display them again and again, each time asking the same question, "How many cards do you see?" The game continues until one of the students notices that each time you shuffle the cards into a different pattern on the ground your hands display (unobtrusively) a different number of fingers. The whole purpose of the short activity is to be aware of what we see and don't see within an experience. It is a simple method of raising conscious awareness within Episodic Memory.

5. The written word

5.1 **Scatter gun:** Have a whole series of feeling words placed on pieces of paper on the ground or around the walls. Give each student ten small pieces of card. Onto each card they write down one feeling associated with their experiences that day. Then on the other side of each card they write ONE sentence describing why that feeling came to mind. For example, a student might write: Trapped – "I felt that I was trapped in a difficult conversation that made me feel really uncomfortable!" After the students have written ten feelings on ten pieces of card, instruct them to spread the cards out before them and form a pyramid of feelings, where the top of the pyramid is the most powerful feeling, down to the four cards (four feelings) at the bottom of the pyramid. They then pick up the three cards uppermost on the pyramid and on a separate sheet of paper write 50 words about each feeling linked to their experience of those feelings. You might then ask them to identify the links between the feeling words they have chosen. See below for a possible feeling pyramid:

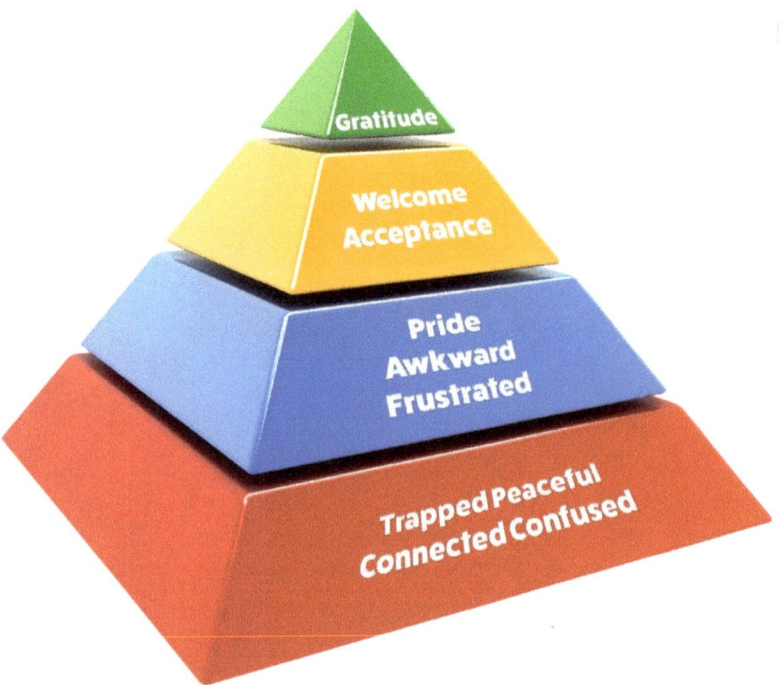

5.2 Guide the students in **writing a letter** to someone they met during their experience. In the letter (a letter that is NOT actually given to the person) that are to describe how they felt meeting that person. Instruct the students to: "Ask them questions, imagine they had asked you questions. Share some of your life story, express gratitude to them ... allow what you want to say to them to arise and be expressed through the letter OR imagine the person you met during the service experience has written you a letter. Imagine you are their hands and heart – writing to you – what would they say to you? Write this letter."

5.3 Instruct students to *keep a journal* of their experiences and reflections. Give them three or four focus questions to write about after each experience. Make sure that the final reflection is, "Any other comments." This allows space for the unexpected to be expressed.

5.4 *Quotations:* Depending upon the theme linked to the experience, produce a whole series of quotations from **Scripture, or the tradition, or a saint, or a hero or a papal document**, that speak to that theme. For example, if it were an environmental theme you could have quotations from *Laudato Si*. Students should then be instructed to walk around slowly and pick up two or three key quotes that speak to their experience and write about 50 words on why they chose these quotes.

5.5 *Lectio Divina:* Scripture can be used in many ways as an aid to reflection. When used, or when our core theology is used, we are beginning to engage in Theological Reflection. In these circumstances Scripture can be used to:

a. **Engage with an *entire Scripture passage***. Who are the characters in the passage? Where are they within the SL experience and why? Use the Lectio Divina process.

b. **Choose *one character from Scripture***. Break open how that encounter between Jesus and that person reflects or speaks to an encounter you have had at the service site (for example Jesus and the widow of Nain, Jesus and the lepers, the blind man, the bleeding woman etc).

c. **Invite students into a *meditation time*** focusing on Jesus in a key scene from Scripture. Encourage them to visualise it, then imagine Jesus meeting them in the scene itself. What does this say to you in relation to your service experience? Once the meditation with key questions from Jesus to the student (in the context of the Scripture scene) is concluded, guide the students in journaling their responses.

d. Similar approaches can be used with **tradition**. Examples of this may include Francis of Assisi meeting the leper, St Peter Claver going down into the holds of slave ships, or St Teresa of Kolkata going out onto the streets.

The examples set out above are merely some of the reflection techniques that the author has used in his practice. Each reader of this guide will have their own ideas based upon their own life experience, their skill set and the context of their Service Learning heightened experiences.

Sharing with your professional peers can assist each of us in picking up wonderful user-friendly reflection techniques. In addition to this, the internet with its numerous resource sites is a helpful resource, and in bookshops there are a myriad of books outlining excellent reflection techniques. There is no need to reinvent the 'Ark'!

CONCLUSION
The Power and Possibility of Service Learning

I met Matthew at the Ozcare having dinner and James Gofton and I both agreed that it was the best chat we had ever had on the van. It was the first and only time a person had really opened up and said what his situation was and told us how he got in this situation. I have experienced the overview of some homeless characters such as they do drugs or get in trouble with family but not the step-by-step progression to their situation. I was grateful that he was happy to not only chat to the two of us but tell us his story.

Journal reflection from Matthew on Eddie's Van.

This study guide began by asking, "How do we learn from an experience?" Too many educational communities just 'do' Service Learning, too few ask HOW do we engage with it so that it is an experience that is truly service and truly learning?

> Psycho-Cognitive Strength: A concept acquires a Psycho-Cognitive Strength when it is experienced and reflected upon in multiple ways over the learning journey of the student. The concept becomes internalised, gaining a universality or an applicability that will be with the student for the rest of their lives.

However, when a community:

i. identifies its core values and associated concepts,

ii. deliberately weaves normative experiences of these values through the culture and curriculum of the community and invites students to reflect on their experience,

iii. identifies and plans for targeted heightened experiences that centre on these values and associated concepts and professionally creates a culture of reflection upon experience around these experiences,

then those core values take on a psycho-cognitive strength in students that will last a lifetime! Service Learning becomes a powerful agent of transformation.

As a student progresses through their years within an educational community and experiences the core values of that community those values gain 'wings', and to varying degrees are personally 'owned'. With repetitive experiences of a concept, held momentarily within Episodic Memory and reflected upon, concepts become more and more owned and part of the internal landscape which is that student's Semantic Memory. In short, that concept is internalised.

Each time a concept is revisited in a deliberate way by educational professionals it has a nuanced additional

layer or facet of meaning to it. Each time, the student experiences that concept slightly differently. Each time, the student has the concept stretched, deepened, expanded upon, in Semantic Memory, experienced in a slightly different way in Episodic Memory. When reflected upon that concept broadens, deepens, and like an accordion effect expands to hold wider meaning. The concept gains a flexibility, an applicability and a universality: we call this psycho-cognitive strength.

Our hope is to graduate young people who have so engaged with the core concepts of the community, and so reflected upon their experience, so that they will graduate with a quite profound level of meaning-making and its associated life skills now a part of them.

Conclusion

Transformation

All education seeks to liberate. All education seeks to plant seeds within the student that ultimately lead the student to taking their place in society creating a better world for all. In a culture of league tables, greed and political, religious, ethnic and social division that threaten the very existence of the planet, true liberating education has never been more important. In this context the Catholic school has a significant role to play.

Core Elements

This guide began by examining the term Service Learning, stressing the importance that it is both Service and Learning. This service seeks to bring about the reign of God within our world, building a society of justice and peace. This service is respect-filled and based upon reciprocal relationships with those served, for "it is in giving that we receive."

But in our Service Learning we are called well beyond any feel-good altruism to a deep learning, a learning where the learner gains skills of critical reflection that

help them see the structural elements leading to much injustice and inequality. The Service Learning journey invites the student to claim their personal agency, noting each of us is called to be agents of change and to make a difference.

Recognising the pedagogical and psychological basis for Service Learning lies in the field of experiential learning, this guide stresses the importance of the Service Learning program working intimately as part of the cultural and curriculum life of the educational community. A healthy community, which this book is written to promote, works hard to name its core values and associated concepts, and then its curriculum. And it culturally maps experiences and learning opportunities where these values 'come to life' through the *life* of the community.

Learning

This guide invites us to go beyond any shallow 'just go out and serve' approach, and instead to also engage deeply in the learning dynamic. As the core values and associated concepts are introduced into Semantic Memory, experienced in Episodic Memory, and then reflected upon, the student not only learns, but grows to 'own' the core values of the community.

Academic Rigour

The psychological processes at play in the Service Learning context are detailed in these pages so that the mentor or educational practitioner can more effectively engage their students in transformational relationships and learning. The phases of the heightened experience are identified alongside both a Service Learning model and the key elements that lead students to ever deeper meaning-making. It is recognised that the Service Learning program is not seeking the 'perfect' experience, but rather to equip students with the necessary skills to engage respectfully, analyse, ask critical questions, and thus learn life lessons, resulting in an increased sense of agency.

Reflection upon experience

The guide stresses the importance of reflection upon experience if true learning is to take place. This continual reflection will engage the meaning-making journey for each student. Using the internalisation process of Alison Le Cornu the guide seeks to assist the Service Learning mentor to understand the processes at play if the student is to journey towards existential change.

Community Values

This guide continually places Service Learning in the wider and more holistic context of a community deliberately engaging with its core values, associated concepts and sense of mission. It is through this context that the concept of gaining a psycho-cognitive strength has been introduced. A student engages with the core values and concepts of the community from their first year through to graduation. They experience these values and concepts in the curriculum, culture and Service Learning program. They reflect on these experiences. In the process of all this their values gain a depth, a universality, and an applicability that the student will carry with them through life.

This is the power and potential of both Service Learning and the Catholic school when it engages with its mission deliberately and professionally.

As Pope Francis reminds us:

> *An evangelising community gets involved by word and deed in people's daily lives; it bridges distances, it is willing to abase itself if necessary and it embraces human life, touching the suffering flesh of Christ in others. Evangelisers thus take on the "smell of the sheep" and the sheep are willing to hear their voice. An evangelising community is also supportive, standing by people at every step of the way, no matter how difficult or lengthy this may prove to be.*

Evangelii Gaudium, No 24.

As Catholic educators we invite our students to come to the other as guest, to choose to be deeply present to the innate dignity of the other as a child of a totally and unconditionally loving God. On this sacred ground of encounter we are profoundly aware of Story. In this sacred space we allow our hearts to open in compassion. All of this, this encounter with the transcendent, with the mystery we call God, leads to a deep, intimate freedom.

As Catholic educators our aim is that our students will experience our schools as evangelising communities and places of encounter, and that long after graduation they will reflect with pride that it is within our communities that they first took on the 'smell of the sheep' and fell in love with the flock.

A Practitioner's Guide to Critical Questions/Statements for Student Engagement

The following questions or statements may be helpful when working with students in Service Learning. They can be raised in various situations:

1. Who is voiceless?
2. Whose needs are ignored?
3. Who makes decisions?
4. At what level are decisions made?
5. Who is unseen?
6. Who is 'out of sight' and 'out of mind'?
7. Who has the power?
8. Who influences the media?
9. Is there a gap between the truth and what the media portrays? Why?
10. Where is the individual in all of this?
11. Whose voice counts?
12. Who is impacted directly by this decision?
13. Who pays? Who really pays?
14. We all pay the cost, but no-one sends the invoice!

15. Who sets the agenda?

16. Who wins? Who loses?

17. If it does not work – why do we do it?

18. "Anyone 'convinced' against his will – is not convinced!"

19. Does 'punitive' punishment work?

20. Rehabilitation or punishment?

21. Who is excluded?

22. Who is included?

23. Who has a seat at the table?

24. Power or empowerment?

25. Economic rationalism?

26. User pays?

27. Survival of the fittest!

28. I win – you lose!

29. "It takes a whole village to raise a child!"

30. The power of perception.

31. Who are the key players in this situation?

32. Who is taken for granted?

33. Who sets the rules?

34. Who decides what game we will play?

35. Who has become an 'it' – of no consequence?

36. Who feels powerless?

37. Who is trapped?

38. Who is empowered?

39. Who has claimed their voice?

40. Who is robbed of their dignity?

41. Who is a pawn in someone else's chess game?

42. Who is the puppeteer and who are the puppets?

43. Who is the outsider?

44. 'He' calls the shots. (Why isn't it 'she')!

45. It is all too much – where do you begin?

46. Does working with the poor isolate you from working with other groups who are also working with the poor?

47. Who holds the 'purse-strings'?

48. What can you see?

49. What do you sense is there, but you can't see it?

50. Why can't you see it?

51. Who allows you to see what?

52. Who are the gatekeepers to this situation?

53. Whose voice is a whisper?

54. Why is that voice a whisper?

55. There is a Church working here but it is not the Sunday Mass one.

56. How do you change the system?

57. Can you change the system?

58. What is the politics of fear?

59. Why is the politics of fear so effective?

60. Where is the Institutional Church in all of this?

61. Does religion play a role in poverty?

62. What role can religion play in keeping people poor?

63. Who is the outcast?

64. What is blocking people's voices?

65. What are the roadblocks?

66. What is fueling the fear?

67. What are the causal factors?

68. What piece of the jigsaw do you think you must have to understand this situation?

69. What labels are limiting?

70. What is 'unfree' in this situation?

71. Who is 'unfree' in this situation?

72. Who is blinkered?

73. What are the blinkers?

74. Whose voice does count and whose voice does not count; the feminine, the earth voice, the indigenous, the peasant, the worker, the disabled, the child …?

75. Who does not want to see?

76. Who is afraid?

77. Who is truly free?

78. Where is the 'face of God'?

79. Where is the 'face of love'?

80. Who are the hands of Jesus?

81. Who reached out?

82. Who has clenched hands?

83. Who is blind?

84. Who is crippled?

Service Learning is a specific professional and pedagogical field within education. To better understand the processes at play within this context the following reading is recommended:

Psychological Processes

Cone, D & Harris, S, 'Service Learning practice: developing a theoretical framework', *Michigan Journal of Community Service Learning*, 1996, pp. 31- 43.

Eyler, J & Giles, D, *Where's the Learning in Service-Learning?* Jossey-Bass, San Francisco, 1999.

Green, P M, 'Service-Reflection-Learning: An Action Research Study of the Meaning-Making Processes Occurring Through Reflection in a Service-Learning Course' (Ed. D), Department of Educational Leadership and Organizational Change, Roosevelt University, Chicago, 2006.

Le Cornu, A, 'Building on Jarvis: Towards a Holistic Model of the Processes of Experiential Learning', *Studies in the Education of Adults*, 37(2), 2005, pp. 166-181.

Price, D F, 'An Exploration of participant experience of the Service Learning program at an Australian Catholic boys' secondary school' (unpublished doctoral dissertation), Australian Catholic University, Brisbane, 2008.

Rochquemore, K A & Schaffer, R. H, 'Toward a Theory of Engagement: A Cognitive Mapping of Service-Learning Experiences', *Michigan Journal of Community Service Learning (7)*, 2000, pp: 14-24.

Seider, S, 'Catalyzing a Commitment to Community Service in Emerging Adults', *Journal of Adolescent Research, 22(6)*, 2007, pp. 612-639.

Youniss, J & Yates, M, *Community Service and Social Responsibility in Youth*, University of Chicago Press, Chicago, 1997.

Spirituality of Service

De Caussade, J P, *The Sacrament of the Present Moment*, Harper Collins, New York, 1989.

D'Orsa, J & T, *Catholic Curriculum: a Mission to the Heart of Young People*, Garratt Publishing, Melbourne, 2012.

Flynn, M, *The Culture of Catholic Schools*, St Pauls Publications, Sydney, 1993.

Gowdie, J, *Stirring the Soul of Catholic Education: Formation for Mission*, Garratt Publishing, Melbourne, 2017.

Hindmarsh, P, *Educator's Guide to Catholic Curriculum: Learning for Fullness of Life*, Garratt Publishing, Melbourne, 2017.

Nolan, A, *Jesus Today*, Orbis Books, New York, 2006.

Normoyle, M C (ed), *A Companion to a Tree is Planted: the correspondence of Edmund Rice and his assistants*, 1810–1842, Dublin, 1977.

Nouwen, H J, *Reaching Out: the three movements of the spiritual life*, Doubleday Image Books, New York, 1975.

Nouwen, H J, McNeill, D P & Morrison, D A, *Compassion; a reflection on the Christian life*, Longman and Todd, London, 1982.

Pagola, J A, *Jesus: An Historical Approximation*, Convivium Press, Miami, 2012.

Helpful terms

Some commonly used terms as they apply in the context of this guide are defined and explained here.

Active Cognition
Occurs when the language, concepts and approaches that populate the Semantic Memory are triggered or activated in the encounter moment.

Agency
The belief and awareness that one can make a difference in the world and contribute meaningfully to society.

Anticipatory Cognition
Where the language, concepts and approaches that are to frame an encounter focus the awareness energy prior to the encounter.

Briefing and De-briefing
Preparation and deliberate focusing of attention to core concepts and outcomes prior to a Service Learning experience and the unpacking of the participant's personal experience after the service experience.

Dissonance
The clash that occurs when one's value and belief system meets people and situations that either bring that system into question or challenge the basis for one's beliefs and values.

Episodic Memory
The memory moment that focuses on the immediate experience and its associated feelings, connections and thoughts.

Experiential Education
The process of learning through experience or learning through reflection on doing.

Grappling
The art of engaging in reflection upon one's experience within the service site/scenario.

Heightened Experiences
An experience that focuses deliberately and specifically on a Service Learning outcome through heightened awareness, targeted concept engagement and focus.

Mission
One's personal response to the call to bring about the Reign of God in the world.

Normative Experiences
An experience that engages with particular concepts directly or indirectly in the day to day life of the community, its culture and curriculum.

Personalisation
The process whereby the client of the service encounter becomes a person with a story, personality and the other facets of personal relationship.

Psycho-Cognitive Strength
The process whereby a concept implanted in the Semantic Memory and experienced and reflected upon in numerous and varied service situations gains a universality and far reaching applicability for life.

Semantic Memory
The memory storehouse containing the mind-maps, concepts, ideas, and information/knowledge gleaned from personal experience.

Service Learning/Engagement
The process of learning through building reciprocal relationships with the other whether the other be a minority group, people from the majority world, marginalised people or the Earth itself. This process requires that the action be one of service or 'other centeredness' and that learning takes place when the action is reflected upon.

Social Analysis
Analysing the factors that make up a social situation or scenario.

Spirituality
How, where and when one finds meaning on life's journey.

Worldview
The personal and conceptual map of the world from which one derives meaning and understanding.

The Educator's Guide Series

The Educator's Guides are designed to provide easily accessible information on mission practice within Catholic Education. They are written by some of Australia's leading Catholic educators who have accepted the challenge of writing at an introductory level in their field of expertise. Excellent mission work is currently being done by Catholic educators. The Educator's Guides draw on and celebrate this work in a spirit of mutual support and dialogue.

Educator's Guide to Immersion for Mission

This *Educator's Guide to Immersion for Mission* provides a unique insight into the multifaceted and complex experience of immersion. Theoretical and theological perspectives, personal experiences and practical examples offer a singular lens through which to view immersion in the context of mission, while at the same time presenting helpful suggestions, frameworks and direction for leaders involved in planning and facilitating immersion trips.

The guide is intended for use by diocesan system leaders, religious institutes, public juridic persons, school leadership teams, mission leaders, social justice coordinators and all those involved in building and strengthening partnerships with rural, remote, indigenous and Majority World communities.

It is anticipated the guide will provide a valuable resource for those wishing to undertake the process of leading others through an experience of personal encounter and cross-cultural engagement, with the ultimate aim of enlivening God's mission in the world today.

Educator's Guide to Mission in Practice

How does the Catholic community understand and commit to the mission of Jesus today? What might missional discipleship look like 'on the ground'?

Mission in Practice addresses these questions. It assists educators to enhance vision and commitment through reflection on their current practice. It also provides an introduction to the scriptural foundations of mission and to normative Catholic teaching. As did Jesus in his time and place, this Educator's Guide contains an invitation to renew vision and hope, and to enter deeply into the grand adventure of missional discipleship in today's world.

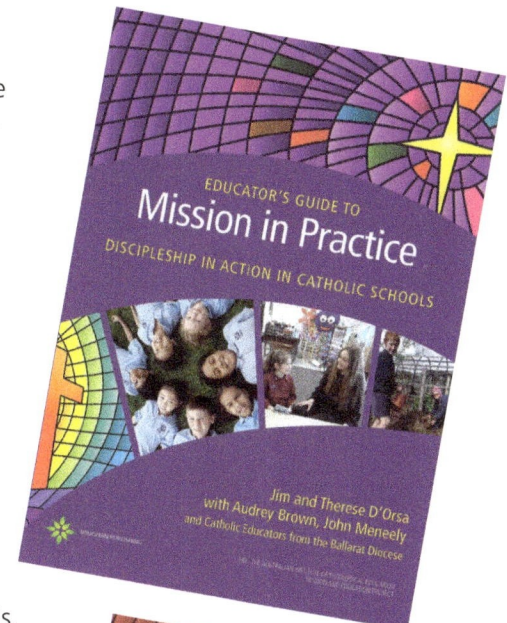

Educator's Guide to Catholic Identity

A practical guide for leaders and leadership teams in Catholic schools.

In the rapidly changing times we live, there is no room for complacency when it comes to Catholic identity issues. Importantly, just how can school leaders and leadership teams address those religious identity questions?

Discover the practical ways Australian schools are evolving their pastoral care programs, curriculum, pedagogy, liturgy and more to enhance their Catholic identity and offer students an even stronger, sustained engagement with their faith.

Drawing on significant research and theoretical reflection, Dr Paul Sharkey examines areas of modern-day school life and considers how each can provide opportunities to create 'Catholic spaces' that draw students in and deepen their relationship with God.

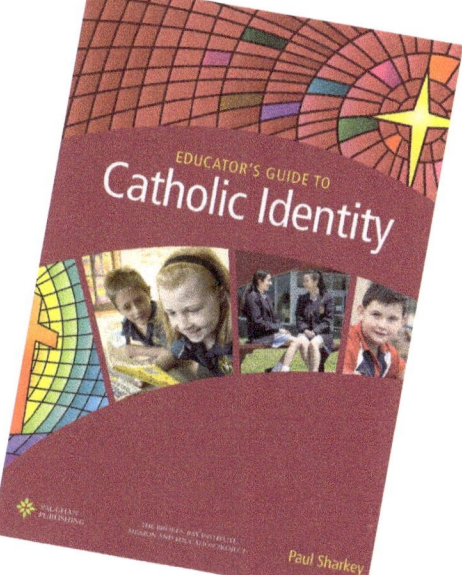

Educator's Guide to Catholic Curriculum

What difference can the Catholic identity of a school make to the way it approaches curriculum? How can the curriculum be 'life-giving' for students in the way Jesus intended when he promised 'fullness of life' for all?

How can Religious Education, the Humanities, the Arts, Maths, Sciences and Technology, Health/PE and Vocational Education be enriched by Catholic faith and life? How can all subjects work together to create an 'ecology' of learning that can help students discern wise life pathways? How can their years of learning the various subjects in school classrooms help them become a 'leaven' in the dough of society and a 'light' for the world?

This Guide offers practical curriculum strategies and school-focused examples from educators in Catholic schools around Australia and New Zealand who are attempting to address these questions.

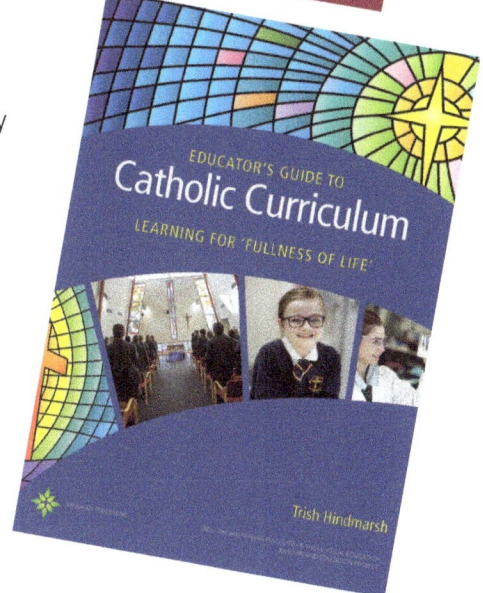

About the Author

Damien Price is an Edmund Rice Christian Brother of the Oceania Province. Damien has worked in Catholic Schools for over forty years.

For the last twenty years Damien has travelled widely throughout Australia and New Zealand conducting professional development and retreat days for the staff of Catholic schools. Damien has also worked extensively with Lutheran Education. Damien's professional development work has focussed primarily on the psychological processes at play, and the skills required, in conducting the school retreat, as well as on similar processes related to Service Learning. On many occasions Damien has been invited by schools to break open a spirituality for the staff of a school that can impact their day-to-day praxis. Damien's Doctor of Philosophy degree explored the meaning-making students engaged in while working with homeless people over an extended period of time. Damien lives in a Brothers' community in Brisbane, Australia.

www.ingramcontent.com/pod-product-compliance
Lightning Source LLC
Chambersburg PA
CBHW040317240426
43666CB00023B/2929